T0149308

SPICE UP
your
SOUL

SPICE UP
your
SOUL

BEAUTIFUL SOUL
BEAUTIFUL LIFE

JENNY PUGH

SPICE UP YOUR SOUL
BEAUTIFUL SOUL BEAUTIFUL LIFE

iUniverse books may be ordered through booksellers or by contacting:

iUniverse
1663 Liberty Drive
Bloomington, IN 47403
www.iuniverse.com
1-800-Authors (1-800-288-4677)

ISBN: 978-1-5320-7963-4 (sc)
ISBN: 978-1-5320-7964-1 (e)

Print information available on the last page.

iUniverse rev. date: 07/30/2019

Contents

Part II

Introduction

This is my second book of the same title Spice Up Your Soul with subtitle Beautiful Soul Beautiful Life.

This second volume will include specific techniques for specific situations that are universal for human beings.

Life is a series of situations leading to success or failures depending on how we handle a situation in any given time and space and on how we define success in a personal level.

In every heart and soul of every human being is a vacuum or a sense of emptiness that needs to be filled in order to live a meaningful hence a happy life.

Money can be a measure of success if your dreams gear toward it. Harmonious marriage relationship is another attractive goal that one may think that it fills the emptiness of your soul. Beauty, health, popularity, meaningful job or career are among life's dreams or achievements that either inspire or pester the soul as the case may be. Yet the feeling of emptiness still persists in one way or another, either most often or in once in a while, in the duration of our lifetime existence regardless of whether we had achieved a goal or we experienced a bitter failure or loss.

The question then is, "is there such a thing that completely fill this vacuum in the soul?"

To answer this question is the objective of this second book where I include specific activities for specific situations that we come across as we journey on in life.

When I was a student in college where I majored in Economics, the first definition that I encountered goes this way "The theories, principles, and models that deal with how the market process works. It attempts to explain how wealth is created and distributed in communities, how people allocate resources that are scarce and have many alternative uses, and other such matters that arise in dealing with human wants and their satisfaction."

In short it said that Economics is a social science that deals with the study on how scarce resources are produced, distributed and allocated to satisfy the insatiable human wants and needs.

Human wants are insatiable, there is no contentment even when they already have achieved a certain goal. Hence as humans we have to deal with our souls, it's the soul that is the true essence of being human and it knows what it wants and needs, it keeps moving up to the next higher levels once a need is fulfilled. It is the soul that connects to the realms of the spirit. The spiritual realm is the director of our destiny. If the spirit is on high level then our lives will enjoy the ride, we will be in the peak of life's achievements in conjunction to our dreams and goals. Even the bible says "don't grieve the spirit" because once grief dwells in your spiritual aspect of existence then everything and in every turn of your life will be miserable. Disease, famine, poverty and the rest of bad lucks happen to you.

As we journey on in life, we encounter so many situations, some are joyful and worth celebrating while others are painful and life changing to the worse. Little do most people know that consciously or subconsciously their souls are the ones inviting all the situations that they happen to be in any given time.

We invite all situations into our lives whether they be problems or joyous happenings. Therefore, it is important that we should feed and nourish our souls with delicious and nutritious food for the soul. And what are those delicious and nutritious foods for the soul?

This book will suggest answers for such a question. Once the soul is healthy then our life's journey will be worth-living in the here and now.

Assertiveness and self-awareness are the basic tools in all the techniques used for the purpose of answering the questions presented here.

If you have read the first volume of this book, you will see some of those situations that I encountered in life and how I deliberately came out from them. In this volume I will discuss certain situations that many if not most people encounter in a lifetime and how to deal with them using the principle of assertiveness and self-awareness.

The Book Spice Up Your Soul

The objective of this book is to inspire and to remind us of our true nature and value as human beings. The author, Jenny Cailing Pugh had spent decades and most of her life searching, researching. introspecting and studying the essence of being human and she had come to the conclusion that the soul is the link that catapult human lives from any misery that humans experience in the material world to the Higher Self and Purpose of life. The book shows the way to create miracles in your individual life when you feel like your situations become so difficult and beyond your control. Once in a while if not often most people would find themselves entangled in life's various problems in any areas such as financial difficulties, relationships in family and loved ones, failures in career and business and many more as you continue to journey in life. Many people just exist and drift by in life without direction because they are disconnected from the essence of their being, they forget, worse have no idea that they have a power within them that is all-knowing and that could create miracles in their lives if only they had learned to reach deep down within them, to the powerful essence of their existence.

Read my book and be blessed.

1

WE ARE ALL SOULS

The soul is the essence of being human. The soul is that part of being human that is precious in the heart of God. This is what Jesus died for.

The soul is the seat of all emotions and it is that part of us that navigate us in life's journey. Whatever and wherever we are in the present are the destination so far that our soul has brought us. The soul knows where we had been, where we are at present and where we are leading. When our soul's task is done in this life it will go back to the Creator, it never dies, our body dies but the soul lives on.

The soul does wonder in our lives if we acknowledge its role. It creates miracles and causes the impossible to happen for our own good. It is the soul that connects us to God or the Spiritual realm of the universe. When things go wrong in life and we feel like there is nothing more we can think or do to change it then that is the time that the soul takes charge and do the supplications in our behalf to the Highest Power that makes everything in this universe possible.

You cannot measure what the soul can do in your life for your own good. It solves your personal problems in all areas, it gives you ideas to change your situation for the better, it guides you and shows you the way for a better if not the best life that you can have, and if you still cannot see the way the soul opens the way for you and leads you on. You cannot underestimate what your soul can do for you, and your soul is you, you are powerful if only you have close connection and relationship with your own soul.

This is the main reason why I have conceptualized and had written the book Spice Up Your Soul. I see the importance of connecting our material life to the inner power within each individual, I had experienced it and I love to share it with people especially to those who have come to me for valuable advice because they had messed their lives deliberately or otherwise.

To spice up your soul means that you acknowledge its power and beauty and to have a harmonious relationship with it in every step of your existence. Be the beautiful soul that you are meant to be as you journey on in life.

2

THE THINKING HUMAN

The Searching Man
This verse is quoted from the Bible. "What is man that Thou art mindful of him? And the Son of Man that Thou visit's him? For Thou hast made him a little lower than angels; And hast crowned him with glory and honor."

Man is a complex crown of creation; Within him are billions of mysteries he himself cannot understand; Even those who spent a lifetime searching for answers can only start with questions and end up full of riddles.

To begin searching the truth from within one's self is tedious enough; How much difficult it would be to search and conclude another human of complexity; It's just enough that a person should watch his own unfolding; To his personal development and natural capacity.

I had tried time and again to search for my own truth consistently; Following my thought processes and flows and formulating my logic and philosophy;

Observing my feelings and emotions in any given situations; Whether I am alone or I am in the midst of a crowd; Whether I am busy or idle. I meditate on my achievements or failures; And searched on my sins of omissions; Compare all these to my present preoccupation; And forecast the future for definite outcome;

Puzzles and questions such as; Who I am; What I am; Where I am; What am I doing in life and in this world as a whole; And why I am doing what I am doing and vice versa;

Bringing out conflicting answers which lead to more questions; The mood and the feelings in any given time; Doing all these lead to more confusion; The more I think, the greater also is the confusion.

Sometimes I want to think that perhaps I will know my own truth by relaxing and doing nothing; Observing Mother Nature's other creations and getting awed at its wonders; Or watching man-made creation and technology as they prosper every day; Surmising what mankind had done and are yet to do; This way I may be able to figure out my role to contribute to the world my own personal value.

I realized that searching for the truth culminates from within; "What is below so is above" is an invaluable fact; To search for an answer is the answer itself; For humans are made to search and search, and crave for the rest of his life on earth; There is no satisfaction for a craving soul;

Even God is craving for love and loyalty; Aren't we human the same? To stop searching for love, beauty, abundance and fulfillment; Is giving up life and returning his breath to the Giver; Craving, desiring, and searching are what humans are meant to be.

Even great thinkers such as Plato, Socrates, Ptolemy, and Pythagoras; And wise men who studied the movements of the sun, the moon, the heavenly bodies and the whole of the universe; Great inventors like Edison, Newton, and Einstein; Richest men like Henry Ford and Bill Gates; Cannot claim that they know everything there is to know in this vast universe; They lived spending all their lives to discover and achieve; Yet they rest in peace feeling that they are not done yet; And were still in the process of searching for what else can they learn and discover in this wondrous universe. Great men who are still alive continue in their search for what else is better than they had already achieved.

The question I must ask myself specifically is; "What am I exactly searching for?" I must be searching in the spirit of joyous exultation; With passion and expectation for the answers I am unfolding; Withe the realization that I can only focus my search for what my heart truly desires; I cannot be searching for everything in this world; For it would only be in vain; I am not made to contain the huge universe inside my limited brain; For this whole universe can only fit in the Mind of the Greatest Intelligence; The Mind that hangs the planets and the solar system and everything that there is; The One who created Mother Nature by just His words.

I can only passionately and continuously search for something unique to me and that which interests me; Such as painting and other hobbies and how to improve my livelihood activities for self-preservation; It's all up to the Greatest Intelligence how I must pursue the desires of my heart; All I do is to "switch on" my connection to the Greatest Source of all wisdom and knowledge; For it knows what is best for me; All I do is to listen and be alert to His guidance and follow it thoroughly; For to live with the

Divine Guidance living within me; Is to know everything there is to know, and which are specific for me;

My tedious searching is now over; For the Source of all Wisdom and Knowledge lives within me.

3

THE ALL-KNOWING SOUL WITHIN US

Even at the time of conception when the physical aspect of our being was in an incomplete stage and was just starting to develop the soul has already find its seat in the heartbeat while the spirit is in the head, this is the reason why these parts of our body are the starting point of our physical development as a human. The soul is already complete within us and it knows every phase of our development as an individual. It is present while the process of knitting every fiber, every tissue and every cell in the physical body was ongoing.

This soul is the connecting element of our being to the spiritual realm of the whole universe. It knows when we are comfortable or are suffering from some discomfort physically even while we are still in the womb of our mothers. It also knows where your life should be going and how you are going to deal with many challenges that would come along, hence when you follow the natural and inherent order of your life as you develop towards adulthood, the soul is happy and will celebrate with you in all your success, you will have a beautiful life with the happy and beautiful soul within you.

On the contrary when you mess up your life through wrong decisions and some mistakes that for you are beyond repair, the soul will be greatly grieved, and you will have a troubled soul, life for you then becomes miserable in all areas. But the soul is not beyond repair, all you have to do is to let your soul redirect your ways. This is not easy to do though especially when you are so set in your crooked ways, the first thing to do is to acknowledge the existence of your soul and pay attention to its longings.

The role of the soul in our life is to keep us moving to the higher purpose of our existence. We as humans should keep looking up to this higher purpose. Majority of us though has no idea what purpose we have in this life let alone looking up and going forward to that upward journey that we are destined to follow. Humans make mistakes but we are also equipped with the ability to stand up every time we stumble even when we fall. The soul is the perfect guiding angel to catapult us to higher grounds, even higher than we can imagine.

Given that you are aware in the first place and had accepted the concept that your soul is your guardian angel who is all knowing about you inside out and from beginning to end, then naturally you would desire to consciously be connected to your soul. Something like you can consult it deliberately in any endeavor you would like to venture in any area of your material life. Is this possible?

This is where positive thinking comes in. What you think is what you become. First be aware of your heart's desire then honor it like it's the language of your soul. We are talking here about lofty desires as against perverted ones. Lofty desires are those that are making you and your own life good and also for the good of everyone concerned. Once you have learned to honor your lofty desire, cement it to your soul by creating affirmations about it. The soul will respond positively and will open the way for you according to your lofty desire.

Miracles happen in your life when you learn to use this process of communication with your own soul.

4

THE UNIVERSAL HUMAN VS. THE INEQUALITY AMONG HUMANS

It is wrong to say that all humans are equal everybody is unique and different from one another; even twins with the same DNA are still unique from each other in many ways especially in terms of their inner personalities.

It is very obvious to see the differences of people including those that come from the same culture, the same community and the same parents.

In terms of achievements and successes in life there are those so-called lucky ones whose endeavors are always followed with success. There are poor people and there are those few really rich people and these are just a few of those we can mention as far as human differences are concerned. So where is the equality here? People are not equal in so many if not most ways.

However, despite these inequalities among humans there is still the real universal components where all humans are being/having in common. To mention just a few, first of all, all humans die in a designated time in the individual level. I say individual level because they don't die together at the same time except for some remote cases such as epidemic, wars or terroristic attacks and accidents, but normally and in general there is a designated time and manner of death for every human and in this case the manner could be the work of the universe, disease, or by any spiritual will for a certain individual.

All humans eat, the food may differ conducive to the territory and availability of the food, and the manner they are prepared or cooked also depend on the socio-economic cultural and territorial situation and condition of an individual or family or community. Socio-demographic-economic conditions attribute to the type of foods being eaten.

Most people who live by the bay where fish is in abundance and easy to get make it their staple food. Those who live in small farms where bananas and local legumes are their products make them their staple food as well.

What is common in human is the mandatory behavior of eating but what is unequal is the kind of food they eat. The kind of food they eat is mostly influenced by cultural and the sociodemographic-economic condition of human beings in the world.

Another basic commonality of human beings is the shelter. All humans, except the nomadic tribes and the homeless need a house for comfort and rest and to bond with the family members. What is common or universal here is the necessity of a home whether it be a castle, a palace or a hut, it is still a home and likewise with the food, the quality and beauty of a home also depends on the socio-demographic-economic condition of the people in question.

The bottom line is that all humans are not equal they differ in many ways than being equal. This fact is the point of discussion in this book, because we are all different from one another and yet we all have the potentials to develop and evolve ourselves into someone or something we deliberately created in our mind so I encourage everyone to use his power of creation so he can choose what kind of individual he should want himself to be and what kind of environment and life condition he should want to be in and to possess.

5

LIFE-CHANGING PROCESSES

Like I always emphasize, life is movement. We cannot be babies forever inwardly and outwardly and we are controlled by time and stages of development and growth.

To begin with, if only we have control in our development perhaps, we would prefer to stay in the womb of our mother where everything is comfort, warmth and abundance of nutritional support from our mothers. But that is not the case of life. If we stop to move on then that is the time we stop living and perish from life.

Life as a movement is an evolution. Human beings develop physically intellectually and emotionally. Learning is experiencing, we learn from our experiences in all areas. Babies learn to walk, learn too that to touch a fire in the candle hurts so he would avoid doing it again. We avoid those things that hurt us that is if we learn. Many people keep doing and repeating those things that hurt them emotionally and their lives eventually.

To dream or create a goal for whatever one wants to become or possess in the future is a dignified human nature. We create ourselves and our future lives starting in the mind. To achieve success in life is a long process. Many people start to dream because of necessity or simply because they want to be somebody who they had seen on TV or anybody they either know personally or through media that they admire. They also want to possess things that they believe would give them a status quo or plainly for comfort and for the love of the aesthetic. There are countless reasons why people dream or wish to be somebody someday or to possess material possessions in the future.

Like I said, dreams do come true but we should understand the process of manifesting our dreams to material reality. We have to remember the philosophy of perfect timing. We are all controlled by time and aside from time there are twists and turns in our life's journey. Most often we reject or fear those twists especially when they are incidents such as death of a loved one and other separations and losses such as losing a job.

Many people are afraid to dream or avoid dreaming big things in life because instinctively they sense that to achieve a dream would mean big sacrifices.

The bottom line is whether we dream or not we grow older, time is moving on and if we do not see our direction we will be pushed by many incidents in life. There are forces in life that push, pull toss or drop us down to the abyss of helplessness. The good news is we are also given the choice which direction to go, and once you have chosen the path you are leading be prepared for many twists and turns ahead, be strong and realize that life is movement, life is learning and life is a series of processes that we have to undergo and once you mastered all these processes then you can say "I am the Master of my own fate."

6

LEARNING TO COMMUNICATE WITH YOUR OWN SOUL

We don't need to be too religious or belonging to any religious sect in order to have close connection with our souls. All that is needed is to be aware and to acknowledge that in essence we are all souls. We can either be a happy and contented soul or a troubled and troublesome one. The Bible and many other History books always have accounts of spirituality in any form of human endeavors, worshipping some sort of gods or the only one Almighty God who is worshipped and followed by generations. Religion or some sort of collective beliefs in some spirit world and beings are evidences that humans are souls. Even the atheists who profess disbelief in God or any spiritual entities in this planet have some feelings of nagging uncertainty or emptiness within them that they cannot definitely define despite their stubborn disbelief in any god or powerful spiritual entity that cause miracles in life in any way and form.

It doesn't matter whether you are a believer or not you are having feelings of emptiness and some longings within you, ones in every while that need attention in one way or another, this is part of being human. Atheists won't accept it as the soul causing them such inner turmoil but it doesn't really matter how one defines it, it exists.

7

LONGINGS OF THE SOUL

The essence of being human is the soul otherwise he will just be a body devoid of emotions and thoughts and cannot even move its own body just like a mannequin.

It is not the purpose of my writings to discuss the details of what a soul is. I presume that it is common knowledge if not common sense that every human is a soul within the physical body.

Emotions and thoughts that drive people to act and behave in certain manners and circumstances are evidences of the soul that is a part, if not the whole of human existence.

The following questions need answers for you to recognize the longings of your soul;

1. What are the good things that you long to become in terms of achievement and personality? What do you desire to become in terms of economic condition or financial stability, material possessions, status quo or social standing, career or profession, reputation, family and social relationships, the list could go on

and on depending on your personal preferences for an honorable and respectable person?

2. What do you love to do, something that you are passionate about where you won't count the time for working on it? What are those things that you are talented in doing?

3. What material possessions do you dream of, house and lot, cars, boats, gadgets? Know what are those things that you really desire to posses including how much income, money you want to receive in regular basis and to save.

4. What kind of relationships do you desire and what kind of people are they?

All these desires are the longings of your soul if you feel and are truly convinced that these are the things that will make your life meaningful. If you can answer them and yet you cannot believe that you can have them all then it's high time for you to consult your Higher Self, your soul, your inner power to make things possible for you. Your Soul knows everything about you and it knows what is best for you. If what you think as your dream does not come true then what is going to happen is better and is the best for you.

8

How to Develop the Faith that Creates Miracles in Your Life

The concept is that in communicating with our own soul, the loudest and most effective medium that the soul can hear and understand in which it responds accordingly is faith, then it is only wise to develop such a faith.

As we journey on in life there are many times that we encounter some sorts of difficulty that come in various forms in any area in our lives. If such difficulty is financial the common solution most people do is to borrow or make a loan. If it is trouble in marital relationships, we tend to seek advice from close friends or relatives, if the situation is looking for a life partner nowadays single people would go to the internet. Whatever the difficulty or situation, average people try to solve their problems through their knowledge or on something that they are used to doing in which most often they don't actually solve the problem they just transfer it to another type of problem which mostly complicates situation in the future.

I would like to mention here a situation as an example. When my second husband Adrian Shiels died, he had no money left because he had been in the hospital for three months, his money was completely exhausted to the penny. In his death I took him to a funeral parlor where his corpse stayed for 21 days because the owner of the funeral parlor won't release the corpse if the bill is not paid completely. The bill was US$2,500 and I had not a penny in my possession, if not for the contributions of my friends I cannot even eat for lack of money to even buy my basic need and I was jobless because I had not worked for five years for taking care of him full time because he was bedridden for years before his demise. After two weeks that my dead was being held in the funeral parlor due to my unpaid bills my best friend, Engineer Veronica Malano Miguel was worried about my situation so she offered to lend me at least $2,000 thinking that maybe the owner will allow me to get my late husband's corpse so I can bury him… My best friend said that she was to sell her car just so she can lend me the money to solve my problem at the moment.

I did not doubt my friend's sincerity but I told her "go spend a vacation to your hometown and forget about my situation, this is my personal problem so let me handle this on my own."

I knew deep in my soul that this situation will resolve itself without creating more problems in the future that may cause conflict with my best friend if I accepted her offer. I just had this kind of faith, an unquivering feeling or sense or intuition if you like that this situation will ease out and everything will turn out alright in my life.

One day I saw outside the office of the funeral parlor

posted that they needed an administrator to run the business then suddenly an idea came to me. I went to the office and talked to the owner asking her to let me bury my dead and in return I made a proposal that I will work in her business as an administrator telling her that I have an MBA and citing my other qualifications to run a business, I further told her that I will work without pay for a period until my bill is fully paid and if she can provide me just something to eat as deduction from my supposed salary. I explained too that I cannot think of some money in the near future to pay my bills so I offer my service. I cannot remember exactly how I explained my situation in details that I noticed she was tearful as she said to me "you are so contrite and sincere, I can understand your intention, no you don't have to work without pay, it's either you work and have your salary normally or you are free to go, take your dead husband, bury him. For me you are cleared, forget about the bills, you touched my soul."

Isn't that another miracle? I owe nobody, no future obligations as far as the funeral bills are concerned. My friends were concerned about me for the difficult situation I was in and they wanted to help, they pitied me, but what they didn't know is deep in my soul I was singing "My Father is rich…, I'm a child of the King, problems resolve themselves and this situation will pass."

Money is very important in life and in the whole world. It solves problems, provides us food and the necessities in life and it allows us to live in comfort; but I can prove to you that FAITH is more important than money. If you have faith your problems will be solved and even money will come to you in abundance. My life is a series of miracles and faith is the reason.

So how did I stumble into this powerful faith? I will tell you my secrets.

I consider myself lucky and blessed to have been raised in a family with parents whose wisdom are unquestionable. Religion aside, I was brought up where in every problem my parents always had answers quoted in the forms of Bible verses, phrases from religious songs and inspiring stories. Just like for example when I was in pain for a long time when I was nine years old because of the wound in my leg that never healed in one year time, my Mom and Dad did everything to cure my wound even brought me to the hospital for dressing by the nurses every morning; I was really crying every day in the duration not only because of the pain but mostly by worrying that it may never go away and I will be forever carrying such a wound. Then one day my Mom said, "that wound will pass just as everything else in life, nothing is permanent." I found it to be true when I just realized one day that my wound was healing at the time when I did not put so much effort to cure it, I just covered it with a band aid or a plaster and left it like it never existed. I did not even bother to clean it even when I had my bath, I didn't bother to strip off the plaster, just left it sticking there until one day after several days when I finally stripped off the plaster, the wound got smaller and was actually healing.

That experience with my wound and what my mother said created in me a sense of trust to natural processes in life.

Trust, belief and faith, these are the main virtues to live a life full of miracles or favorable coincidences. Those I call miracles must be interpreted by many as coincidences, if so, then let's create those favorable coincidences in all areas of our lives and this could be possible through the virtues I just mentioned.

Now going back to the topic of how to develop the faith that creates miracles.

If you are the type who is not comfortable repeating inspiring words and quotes in a daily basis then you better start it now because this is the first step to develop the faith that creates miracles. Do it in the spirit of fun, meaning do not push or force it into your mind if you cannot believe it.

For example, there is something, say a dress you would like to buy and you really like it but you cannot afford it for the moment…say to yourself "that dress or something better is mine NOW". In your mind clatter there is a taunting laughter which says, "what a crazy woman, I am just fooling myself" or "because I am poor so I just dream the impossible… look at you, you know the truth, you have no money for that so how can it be yours now, stop that foolishness"

You sense the clatter alright and acknowledge it but don't argue even in your thoughts just imagine how you feel when you actually own the dress, feel the comfortable feeling while wearing it, see the details, the color and the design, do this just in a flash then forget all about it." In this way, your soul got the message and God knows how this dress or something better would come to you in perfect timing.

Next is make it a habit to affirm what you really want, the affirmation may be as simple as I am beautiful, I am rich, well and happy. I am getting smarter, smarter and smarter every day, I now have a monthly income of $10,000; just about anything you want, acknowledge the mind clatter but don't argue then proceed to enjoying the scenario when you actually be that person who in your dream.

And last, be wary on your thought processes, when negative thoughts speak so loudly within your mind, say the opposite, for example you have an enemy who to you she looks so ugly and is so dumb and stupid. Say the opposite like "she is actually beautiful because she is part of this beautiful universe and she is bright in her own right," The idea is to change your belief system and impression to something more beautiful and favorable to you and to everyone concerned. Make it a mental habit until your mind gets familiar with such a wonderful mental attitude and habit.

The whole idea of developing the faith that creates miracles in your life is to discard any negative thoughts and replace them with positive and creative ones. Constant practice through repetition of the exercises makes perfect. The changes, coincidences and miracles that are going to happen in your life is personal to you. The stronger the faith you have developed the more miracles happen in your life.

9

HOW TO HAVE COMPLETE CONTROL OF YOUR LIFE

To live the life that you really want is the best life that you can have. This is the kind of life where there is nobody else and nothing can make you a servant or a slave. You only do things that you really want to do and nobody would oblige you to do anything against your will. This is the kind of life where you are not pressured or burdened or stressed by anything or anyone because you are in control.

You may ask, how could this be possible when you are working in a certain company?

There are countless situations in life that are controlling your life. Just like your job, even if you don't feel like going to work you are forced to go to work otherwise you will have no income to support your needs and your family.

We cannot control other people, family peer groups and the bosses in your work place. If there is anything in life that we can control, it's ourselves; we can control the way we think.

There are three basic and important principles to

consider if we want to control our lives and that nobody else to control us. Remember that nobody and nothing can control us if we don't allow them. The first principle is called Beingness next is Doingness and lastly Havingness, in this order.

In the material perspective success is measured by how much money and material possessions you acquired; this is called status quo. This may be true but remember that we are not just material, we are spiritual too and most importantly we are souls. Material possessions in abundance are not enough to make us happy in this life, in fact they can corrupt us if we neglect our spiritual component.

I will discuss here the three principles that govern our lives in order to have complete control of our individual life.

Beingness: This is self-knowledge or self-knowing. If there is any knowledge in this world that is so important it is the knowledge about you, yourself. Know your deepest desires, know what you really want, your needs and what you really want to do. What is that something that attracts you to do and that you know you won't get tired doing it every moment of your life. Discover that from within you and then improve it and harness your expertise in that area.

Doingness: Once you are sure with what you really want for yourself and what you want to do then just do it. This will be the perfect time for you to study and learn about the details and facts about the job that interests you.

Havingness: Success in material possessions and money will just come naturally to you once you do the first two steps.

When you do something because everybody else is doing it you will find out eventually that you lost interest in them and you will feel like you are tied down to what you are doing, you are controlled by the situation that comes along in doing what everybody else expects from you. You are in control of your own life if you know what is best for you or what you like most and do it accordingly.

10

THE VACUUM OR SENSE OF EMPTINESS IN ALL HUMANS

At the dawn of the social science of Psychology it was defined to be the study of the soul until scientists found out that the study of the soul cannot be a scientific study because they cannot put the soul in the laboratory. A scientific study should be measurable and must be subjected into scientific experiments. So, they change the definition into a study of human behavior which is now measurable, they can create theories and experiments through the tangible human behaviors by comparison and many more controlled situations so that they can draw conclusions based on their scientific methods.

The soul is the essence of being human and this is one of the most crucial components of being human. It is the soul that determines what kind of life you are going to live in the physical world. It is all knowing, it knows where you come from, where you are going, what you deserve in life, what you are supposed to do and it is the seat of the so-called vacuum of humanity or the sense of emptiness.

This soul is the very reason why people follow a religious belief, it's the soul who knows the emptiness within a human being and if you don't listen well to what it is saying to you, you will be lost in life and your spirit will trouble you. There are those so-called troubled soul individuals because they are disconnected to their own soul, the real human that dwells within them. It is the soul that lift our voices to the God of the Universe, that God who is all-knowing and all-powerful to change the directions of an individual's life.

We don't need to be so religious in order to be closely connected with our souls, we are the souls after all. To be closely connected with our souls require the following steps:

1. Know the contents of your thoughts at all times;
2. Hear what your thoughts are saying concerning certain objects, certain people, certain situation and actions, and most importantly your concept about you as a person;
3. Acknowledge your desires and aspirations, define them and honor them;
4. Congratulate yourself and appreciate your soul, yourself actually for giving birth or for having the ability to dream something good or for desiring lofty things for yourself.
5. Put the right words by writing down affirmations or think of those affirmations consistently.

Like I always said, the effort is from within.

11

THE EFFORT IS FROM WITHIN

In life's journey we encounter countless challenges and sometimes problems and situations that never go away. There are lots of happy moments alright but they are just incidentals such as celebrations of various types like birthdays, graduations, Christmas, New Year, among others. But the real celebration should be from within, something like you always have reasons to celebrate life regardless of situations.

Life continues and it should be lived by the moment rather than just floating with the waves of time without concrete direction. The journey itself is the destiny, it's a moment by moment living, the here and now.

What life situation are you in now? Do you have reasons to celebrate? to be happy in this very moment? Or does your mind dwell on poverty, your bills, your unsatisfactory job or financial difficulties? Do you feel insecure with your romantic relationship? Is your mind full of worries just about anything? Such mundane worries as what to cook and eat in the next meal, what to wear in any given momentary situation?

If you allow your mind to worry about anything then you are not living life you are pestered by miseries that life could find, there are millions and billions of them because they multiply by the moment. Once you start worrying about something that worry will invite all its relatives and clans and they multiply by the moment until you are drowned into the abyss of helplessness.

Take for example a young person who had just graduated high school and desires to proceed to study in college but his parents are poor and can't afford to send him to school. He had this strong desire to become a degree holder because he thinks that this is the only way to improve his life situation, but his problem is he had no money to support such a dream; he was thinking of maybe to work and study at the same time but another problem comes up, what work could he find, will the employers be kind to him, will it be possible for him to do these at the same time, where will he stay since college is far from his hometown, will the money he would earn be enough to pay rent and bills and his daily needs such as food, transportation among other expenses and to support his study...and so forth and so on. Before seeing himself in his mind's eye his graduation day he is already blocked by all the worries that multiply themselves by the moment, therefore the decision would be just to forget about such foolish dream, it's just impossible in his situation then he feels undeserving for anything he would dream of and that he is just a failure in life. He accepted his defeat before he can even try to do one step towards the achievement of his goal.

Let's now survey the fate of another young man with the same dream and financial difficulty in the family. This man has a very strong faith that is rooted in his soul. He knows the problems surrounding his dream but he does not focus on them. He gets a pencil, color sticks and a big board and draw a young man wearing the toga on his graduation day. He writes under the drawing "Congratulations (writing his name, let's just call him John...it's your graduation day today, you are a successful man that you deserve to be" Then he posts this board on a wall inside his bedroom where he can see it all the time that he is in his bedroom. He smiles every time he sees it and he feel happy looking at his drawing. Then one day their family had a visitor, an old family friend of his parents. The bonding was wonderful where in the end the visitor asked John if he is interested to work as his assistant in his business while he goes to college at the same time. Lucky John? Well we won't know what our soul would do for us. John's soul sees his colorful drawing of himself as a successful young man and every time John smiles at his drawing and feels happy seeing it, the soul feels the same and will do everything to make such a dream come to reality; that is how powerful the soul is. Our soul knows another soul who could supplement your need and it causes these two souls to meet. Just have faith in your Higher Self, which is the soul, it knows something that we do not and cannot. Humans are shortsighted but we have a soul that knows everything because it is connected to the spiritual realm of our existence.

Life should be full of joy from within regardless of any temporal situation.

12

AFFIRM YOUR TRUTH TOWARDS A HAPPY LIFE

What is inside our head that dominates our mind in a moment by moment basis and in every day of our lives are reflected in our material lives. If our minds are preoccupied with thoughts of discontent in any area and form and is full of complaints and criticism for other people and other social institutions and government so is our lives be poor, unhappy and ridiculously miserable.

What exactly is the kind of life that you would like to live? You may answer, I just want to be happy but it seems that happiness is elusive. One day you are happy and full of laughter but even moments of happiness pass like bubbles.

If the reason for that momentary happiness is because you receive a big amount of money then such happiness will pass as quickly as the money. If the reason for that momentary happiness is because of the presence of any person that is dear to you then such happiness will quickly pass too because people in our lives come and go. People in our lives, just like money, come and go. If the reason for your momentary happiness is because you achieved something that you had been pursuing and that you are accorded honors and awards, this too will pass, every moment of celebration in our life's journey is momentary and these moments are all temporary. Even so-called successes in any endeavors such as graduations, career success, business success and anything that humans strive to achieve will all pass, even humans ourselves pass away from this life.

So, what's the point in living, what is the meaning of life, what is permanent?

The only permanent thing in life is the soul, it never dies and continues to exist through eternity.

King Solomon in the Bible says that everything under the sun is vain. In this case what is important for any human while living this life? Money? Loved ones? Family? Success? What are people in general busy about in their everyday life?

The most important thing that any human can possess in this life is joy and happiness. If you learn to embrace life, all the joys and reasons for happiness and even all the griefs and pains and yet happy to be alive and to continue moving on with a melody in your heart for any situation then that is the true meaning of life.

Happiness that emanates from within instead of being caused by any outward reasons is pure joy in the soul that never dies.

A happy soul brings into our lives all the outward reasons to be happy. We will acknowledge the countless blessings in the past, in the present and that are yet to come when we have a happy soul.

Now, our topic is to affirm your truth for a better life. By this we have to have a specific statement that make your life a life filled with happiness and joy that emanates from within. The objective is to feel the joy, not just think of the happiness; to feel is the key.

The suggested affirmation is; I am a beautiful and happy soul. Or to be specific you can write in this form of affirmation; I, Jenny, am a beautiful, healthy, wealthy and happy soul. Write in first, second and third person, repeat 20 times a day for 28 days.

13

CORE BELIEFS

Your core belief is the railing you lean on in life's journey. When everything else fails your core belief system is your saving factor to let you move on and go on in your rightful destiny. Core belief is actually faith in the true sense but faith has a religious connotation so it's safer to use this phrase for the purpose of this discussion.

A strong core belief within an individual is a principle that he had established within himself because he had proven it to work for him in many situations in his life. A person with strong conviction cannot easily be swayed by anything that does not jibe with his core belief. It is his principle that he lives by in everything that he does. But then we should check what are these core beliefs that we keep within ourselves. There are constructive and destructive core beliefs, I will discuss later the different core beliefs and differentiate them from the other. There are core beliefs that create miracles in our lives while some, if not most of these beliefs that people keep within them lead them to destruction.

What are the longings of your soul? The soul is the seat

of all longings and desires. What is that part of your life that you want to improve? Or worse that you feel you are missing out.

The environment and culture are the basis of the longings of our soul. The words we hear, the objects we see, our socialization process with the family, peer groups and other people we associate as we go along in life influence the kind of longings we harbor in our soul. Our five senses are the windows and gateways to the soul from the material world. But our inner responses to all the things we outwardly experience determine the direction of our lives, hence we can say we create our own destiny in life.

Many people (souls) drift in life with no direction worse is it is directed toward self destruction. We have a responsibility to tame our soul so that it can guide us to the right direction in life's journey.

Is there hope for transforming this kind of life into something beautiful? The answer is, it's never too late for as long as you are alive.

Remember that it is your core belief system that brought you to where you are now because you become what you believe in the deepest sense.

Here are some steps to transform your life:

1. First check your belief system. What do you believe about you as a person, about money, about job and work, about love and relationships, about spirituality that includes God and religion and about anything that lead to success and a happy life?

2. Once you discover the beliefs that are destructive to you, embrace the constructive beliefs and

discard the destructive ones then apply the Healing Affirmations that I am going to discuss in my next video.

3. Develop and strengthen the new core beliefs…as I said core beliefs is faith. Once your faith is strong, everything will be possible to you. You will be creating miracles in your life.

Therefore, the aim of every human should be to strengthen his constructive core beliefs so that his life would be a life full of miracles.

Next time I will be discussing the differentiations of destructive and constructive core beliefs and the Healing affirmations.

14

TWO MAJOR TYPES OF CORE BELIEFS: DESTRUCTIVE AND CONSTRUCTIVE.

As you know so far from our recent discussion, a core belief is that most powerful part of your being that seats in the core of your soul. No matter how you look, whatever your health condition is, and whatever the condition of your life in all areas are determined by the type of core beliefs that you keep deep inside you. It is not necessary that you are aware of all the core beliefs that live within your soul structure but looking at the condition of your health, beauty, and the condition and situation of your life in all areas will show the type of core beliefs that are ruling your life. The type of belief you keep cause you success and happiness in life or may bring you all miseries and destroy you eventually.

Let's survey first the destructive core beliefs. Destructive core beliefs are those beliefs that block you from success in any endeavors you take in life; in a sense they are bad luck beliefs that you had not realized you had been dragging with you throughout your life. If you are aware of these types of core beliefs, would you still continue to keep them?

Some examples of bad luck core beliefs that cause you to live a miserable life:

1. I am not beautiful, maybe I am sexy or not really ugly but surely not beautiful enough to my liking.
2. I am not really good, I just pretend to be good so that people won't dislike me but I am actually a liar, a pretender.
3. I am not as smart as my sister or any friend but so what?
4. I am poor, I come from a poor family so no matter what I do, I stay poor.
5. Life sucks, everything in life is just misery.
6. Life is full of problems.
7. I am just born unlucky in everything. I had learned to accept this fact.
8. I just cannot do anything right.
9. I am full of inadequacies in anything I try to do.
10. My Mom and Dad said that I am sickly ever since I was a baby and that is true.
11. Hard work is the key to success.
12. I am lazy.
13. I am not really lovable but I try hard to be one.
14. Rich people are arrogant.
15. I don't really want to be rich, that is impossible.
16. Money is the root of all evils.
17. Beautiful people are boastful, I don't need to be one.
18. Best friends are best enemies, I don't need one.

19. Happiness is a strange word; it does not exist.
20. Love is a foolish word; people are naturally dishonest.
21. I am always in need of money, who is not or everybody is.
22. Men are liars.
23. Women are untrustworthy.
24. Children are spoiled, they should not be given anything they demand.
25. Spouses cheat on each other.
26. Wives only want their husbands' money.
27. Husbands are selfish.
28. Miracles never happen, not to me.

There are countless of these types of destructive core beliefs that rule the world, I cannot mention them all, no wonder billions of people live miserable lives. If you have all of them or any three of these in the list then you better check yourself, they are bad lucks that come from within you, they block you from becoming a wonderful person or for having a good life.

Now before we go to the healing affirmations let us look into what constructive or creative core beliefs are. Constructive core beliefs also seat in the core of your soul and they have been there creating patterns of good luck and miracles in your life. Do you have many miraculous events in your life? Be happy, you have a guardian angel keeping watch over you in every turn of your life and that guardian angel are your constructive core beliefs.

In my next video I will discuss constructive core beliefs which are actually healing affirmations. I will deal on how to discard the destructive core beliefs that had been operating in your lives replacing them with constructive core beliefs. To cement these constructive core beliefs into your soul will be the aim in the next topic.

15

CONSTRUCTIVE CORE BELIEFS AND THE HEALING AFFIRMATIONS

My last discussion was about destructive core beliefs that are embedded in the structure of the soul and that these are like cobwebs of a monstrous spider that creates a stable habitat and expands to create clans if left unattended. Can you imagine your soul in such a condition, the habitat of a dreaded monstrous creator of bad lucks in your life?

Like I said destructive core beliefs are bad lucks that we drag along as we journey on in life. They are so powerful that they can camouflage like angels of light yet they actually block you in your pursuit for a good life in all areas and you will one day realize that you are in a great despair. These destructive core beliefs attack the person anytime and in any area of his life.

Before going to the constructive core beliefs let's talk about how we were able to possess these core beliefs in the first place.

Newborn babies are all innocent in the sense that

their soul is pure and unblemished from any influences in the material world, physically, mentally and emotionally. Although there is a new study which theorizes that babies inside the womb can sense the emotional state of the mother and that it could affect its personality, but then when it comes to core beliefs we deal with the active participation of the baby with its physical environment. That sense of the baby inside the womb is a passive one where he is not involved in using his will; we are talking here about the active and willful involvement of the baby for him to start formulating a certain core belief within him as the case may be. These beliefs begin with observation, active or passive, observation comes from seeing, hearing and sense feeling.

The five senses are the gateways to the soul and as the baby grows, he learns many things from the environment through the use of all its senses. He will learn which taste to prefer, what sound and sight to enjoy or to dread. It is through this learning process that humans start to accumulate the core beliefs that go straight to the soul hence it is impossible for us to know every core belief that thrive in our soul.

Given this premise that it is impossible to know or be aware of all those destructive core beliefs within us then we don't need to know the unknown unless you are professionally trained along that line, but lucky for us we have a soul that knows everything and all we can do is to trust our souls, have faith in that major part of our being who is all-knowing of all that we are, past present and future.

To trust our all-knowing soul will then be our greatest goal if we want to heal ourselves or to unburden ourselves from the loads of bad luck that we are carrying all the while.

Taking some of the examples of destructive core beliefs n my previous article "Two Major Types of Core Beliefs; Destructive and Constructive", in the following I will use them as the bases for the healing affirmations:

Destructive core beliefs:
1. I don't really want to be rich, that is impossible for me.

Note: Many people have this kind of core belief although secretly they wish they were rich and yet they cannot believe that they can be rich. When they start to think of getting rich many clatters in their mind would start to attack them such as "stupid, you are not going to get rich, you don't know how unless you win the lottery jackpot but even that is close to impossible." In this case there is a conflict between your wish and your core belief, they don't agree so you will justify yourself by saying I don't really want to be rich, that is just impossible for me."

The question then is how to heal this kind of core belief so that the wish will win over the belief?

This is one example of diagnosing your one particular destructive core belief. You have to acknowledge that you have this sort of belief within you. You also have to acknowledge your wish or desire. Honor your desire, uphold it because that is really what you want. Enumerate all the good things you experience when you are rich enjoy them in your mind. Each of us has a definition for rich, what is your definition, make it clear in your mind saying "because I am rich, I have cash balance to my name of the amount, say $5M. The point is empowering your wish so that the destructive core belief will die a natural death, you won't hear it clattering in your mind anymore.

But this is easier said than done. Your belief has been living within you and has been influencing your way of thinking and behavior since time immemorial so you have to do a lot of effort that emanates from within. The mind works effectively in opposites, antonyms, positive versus negative. So, in this destructive core belief which says "I don't really want to be rich, that is impossible for me." Say the opposite "I really want to be rich; everything is possible for me." Then change it into an affirmation form which is the present. "I am now rich; everything is possible for me." If you can believe in this statement you will be rich eventually according to your definition.

The problem here is you cannot really believe it to happen. Then if you cannot believe, don't force yourself do some very effective technique so that eventually without you even realizing it you already had believed in the statement but then you are already rich when that day comes.

What you do here is develop the faith in that statement. Write it down in the spirit of fun twenty times a day for 28 days in first, second, and third person such as this: Let's say your name is Jenny write it this way;

First person: I, Jenny, am now rich, everything is possible for me.

Second person: You, Jenny are now rich, everything is possible for you.

Third person: She, Jenny, is now rich everything is possible for her.

I know this sounds crazy but try that crazy part of you, that's how it works miracles in your lives. You can also do the same process in any of your wishes and desires in areas of education, relationship, career and just about anything that matters to you. Let your soul do magic for you.

16

CORRELATION BETWEEN AFFIRMATION AND FAITH

Let's get serious about faith with the understanding that faith is the loudest medium of communication that our soul can hear and respond according to our desires; and once the soul responds the processes leading to the miraculous, meaningful and happy life that you deserve will begin.

To be successful with any goals in life that you desire to pursue is a long process, success does not come in the instant you have thought of it, although thoughts and ideas in any instant should be honored, but you have to go through all the details of your personal definition of success then you try to figure out the how the when and the how much and everything else that is meaningful to you in relation to such a goal that will lead to your success and achievements.

One of the general definitions of affirmation is "a statement or proposition that is declared as true" "It helps eliminate negative and limiting beliefs and transforms your comfort zone from a limited one keeping you trapped in mediocrity to a more expanded one where anything is possible. It helps to replace your *"I cant's"* with *"I cans,"* and your fears and doubts with confidence and certainty."

Given the definition of affirmation as mentioned above is true then we can already see why affirmation is correlated with faith. Faith is defined as believing in the soul level those things or concepts that are not yet seen or heard.

The soul of the believer sees through his mind's eyes the objects and scenario that he desires for his life, hear those words he deliberately chooses to hear inside his mind. In this case affirmation is the perfect tool to strengthen faith.

When the mind becomes accustomed to perfectly worded affirmations in a regular basis, faith gradually grows and blossoms into a very strong and powerful medium to communicate with the soul.

While the objective of affirmation is to develop faith, faith's objective is to effectively communicate with the soul. Communicating to the soul is just like talking to another person quietly or in writing, most effective way to communicate with the soul is to state your reaction to the present situation that cause you worries and anxieties and with faith surrender such situation to the all-knowing part of your being. The answer is immediate in the sense that your faith gives you a feeling of certainty and assurance that your communication to your soul will bring you favorable results in as far as the content and subject matter of the present communication.

Life is a journey and a series of incidents along the way. Your all-knowing soul is the one that knows where you are at present, where you had been and where you are leading; hence constant and active communication with your own soul will give you assurance that you will never fail, never be lost and if you falter along the way it will let you stand, strengthen you and guide you to the right direction. We are the soul, our essence is it, we have power within us just let it work through faith as being developed through affirmation.

17

HOW TO ACTIVATE THE POWER THAT LIES DORMANT WITHIN YOU

Why would so many people feel so helpless in many situations in their lives? In life we encounter several situations where we have to make decisions and these decisions oftentimes lead us astray. It's okay to make mistakes or make wrong decisions, this is part of being human but we are lucky despite the wrong decisions we had made in the past because we are also equipped with the ability to correct them and to turn away from the path of total destruction. We have the ability to catapult from poverty, from abusive relationships, and from any problematic life situations where we ourselves brought into our lives because of wrong decisions. We have to take responsibility of any situations we are suffering instead of blaming other people or anyone else even ourselves. We made the wrong decisions, we made mistakes because that was the only way we can see in the moment but it won't make things better if we blame ourselves or others. The best thing to do is to acknowledge the mistake, forgive yourself and others then change your flow of thinking, your habits and the direction of your life.

I just had a conversation yesterday, with one of my best friends and ex co-teacher Violy. In that conversation she said to me "I had noticed even long time ago that you can make impossible things possible for you." This statement is not just from her, all my best friends in the past would really think that I have the ability to change my life. Like so many people I had been into situations where problems in all areas attacked me because of wrong decisions but when I discovered that I have a power within me that can change my life's direction everything changed easily. All of us has this power within us that turns the impossible to possible; you just have to discover those powers and activate it.

Do you want to change a situation in your life or change the total condition of your life? Then here are some suggestions:

1. Remember you are a soul and this soul is powerful to create miracles in your life;
2. Acknowledge the bad situation that trap you such as poverty, joblessness, abusive relationship among others;
3. Activate the power that lies dormant within you.

The question remains, how do I activate this power within me to better my life?

Poverty and bad life condition are not determined by relationships and the place where one lives. Why are they poor in this very rich country? Many young Filipina ladies would risk destroying their reputation by marrying an old American guy just so they can come to America and start building their lives whereas this born American lady is suffering from poverty and finds life so boring. Bad life conditions are the results of the mental attitudes and orientations of an individual therefore it's a person's responsibility to change his life's destiny by starting the changes from within...activate your inner power, only you can do it.

Here are some suggestions to activate your power.

1. Acknowledge the presence of your soul within you by this affirmation; I am a precious soul;
2. Have constant and consistent sincere conversations with your soul in the form of affirmations;
3. Converse with your soul daily, even in thoughts only, give it positive words such as faith, abundance, beauty, happy, success and the likes;
4. Discard negative thoughts and replace them with positive ones;
5. Pay attention to your feelings and honor your desires.

18

DESTINY

I choose this topic for my discussion for today as I am inspired by the questions of my friends about what their destiny in life would be. Nowadays you can find in the internet so many fortune tellers and psychic who would tell you about your destiny. In fact, I receive dozens of emails from fortune tellers and psychics who are trying to convince me to pay them for their services to tell me about my destiny. They all sound very convincing they say they will do rituals and some sort of incantations to the universe and spells to help me make my wishes come true, they even try to sell me some powerful tiny artifacts to use as talisman or charms to attract wealth or my perfect match in a romantic relationship. They show testimonies of those they say benefited from their services and are now living the lives of complete happiness having their wishes come true in the areas of love, relationships and wealth.

These fortune tellers and the likes prosper in their careers because many people would like to have a change of their life's destiny from what they feel is unbearable and is different from the kind of life that they dream of. This fact is a proof that many people want to know their destiny in life.

Let's face it, nobody can tell you what your destiny in life is. Only you can tell because only you who can know yourself from inside out. Where you are and what you are in the present is your destiny. If you don't like your life now in terms of wealth, love relationship, family relationship, home situation and domicile, career and others such as comforts in life then you should ask yourself, what am I doing in my life?

Nobody else can create a perfect destiny for yourself, only you. It's just like nobody can eat the food for you, only you can eat your food to nourish your body. Nobody can take a major examination in order to pass for you, you take it yourself.

Destiny is a product of your dreams, your desires, your decision-making, your emotional set-up, your mental orientation and culture.

It is also a product of your gene, upbringing and education or learning processes. You are the creator of your own destiny, a co-creator of your own life. From the womb, God's miraculous ways take care of your development but once you are out into the world you have to effort physically, emotionally and even as babies you start to demonstrate some tricky behaviors to attract attentions especially when you feel some discomforts or dislike just about anything in your immediate environment.

To sum up: Your destiny is your life now, the present life, you had created it knowingly or unknowingly as you live your life in every stage. You can change your destiny by changing your mental orientation, nobody else can do that for you.

19

HOW TO CREATE YOUR OWN DESTINY

This topic now is a continuation to my discussion last week. The reason for this topic to come up is that I received some messages in my messenger asking if there is a specific method to change one's destiny. The answer is yes and no.

What I am presenting here is a method in general but they are subject to modification in accordance with a person's total personality structure. There is no exact science to perfectly study a human being and his life. Even Psychology can only study what is observable and measurable in human behaviors. At the onset of Psychology as a science it attempted to define it as a study of the soul but no one can see the soul and therefore it cannot be observed and measured hence it shifted to studying behaviors instead because behavior can be observed and analyzed.

No one knows exactly what the future is for a certain individual but we can predict our own personal future in a general manner by knowing ourselves and our own way of thinking and reacting to any given stimulus in a given time.

Here are some basic guidelines to create your own destiny.

1. Know yourself, what you desire, how you respond and react to various situations in life; know your strength and weaknesses, make a thorough and comprehensive study of your past behaviors in various situations and with various types of people you had encountered. Know what you enjoy doing, know your preferences in terms of your life's status, is it more on having plenty of money or is it more in popularity. There are a lot of things to study about ourselves. No one else can make a thorough study about you but you, yourself. If you allow other people to study about you there would always be a bias, a prejudice because they will study you according to standards, not you as a unique person. Know what you truly believe in all areas of your life.

2. Dream big for yourself. Dream what you would like yourself to become. Dream what you would like to do. Dream what valuable material things you would like to possess in life, dream how much money you would like to possess in the near or some distant future. Dare to dream.

3. Study and learn how you are going to make your dream come true both in your imagination and in your action. Remember the effort is from within…. Believe because what you believe becomes you.

The preceding are just general suggestions, each person is unique and can create his own destiny according to his conviction. The bottom-line is that you should be aware that you can create your own destiny and that you have the ability and power to do it...trust yourself.

20

TAMING THE RESTLESS
SOUL WITHIN YOU

I n the structure of being human there is an inherent emptiness or vacuum or longing embedded in the soul that demands to be filled. In the spiritual point of view, these qualities are intended by the Creator for humans to use as a railing to live by in a moment by moment experience of existence. The quality of life that an individual is experiencing depends so much on how he handles the longings of his soul in every step of his journey and development in life, and how he dreams or make goals to fill such emptiness.

People are as complex as the universe. This vacuum or feelings of emptiness are determined by two major influences namely the inherent or genetic nature of a person and the culture or the environment. The intensity and the individual responses of a person to these natural longings of the soul are dependent on these two components of the person in question. Some people are more focused on things that are meaningful to them or those they deem important for their well-being and they know what to do with it, while others and these are the majority try to fill their emptiness with mundane and temporal excitement.

Those people who are focused acknowledge their mistakes and wrong decisions then learn from their mistakes and eventually find ways to drop those mistakes and start changing their ways for the better. We may not be able to correct those mistakes and damages already done in the past but we can leave them behind and change our focus to the new way of living our lives.

To tame our restless nature is not to fill the emptiness but to familiarize with our own individual nature and desires. To familiarize with ourselves and with what we really want in life decreases the intensity of our longings. We often long for something that we don't really need or that they just cause us stress and problems in the long run.

We may honor our desires but one of the wisest virtues to embrace should be to learn how to detach ourselves from what we consider valuable to us. To detach means that we take things easy and let our soul work for us because it knows what is best. To detach means to surrender our desires to the all-knowing soul that lives within us; this way we unburden ourselves from working too hard to get what we want.

To tame our restless soul therefore is not to fill the vacuum within us by temporal excitement but to familiarize ourselves with the longings of our souls and to surrender to and trust in its ability to bring to us what really matter in our personal lives.

21

THE VALUE OF FORGIVING

Anger, hatred, jealousy, envy, remorse, feelings of inadequacy, humiliation, feelings of being abused mentally and physically, feelings of being cheated on or betrayed, and other painful feelings slowly eat the soul to death if not checked and corrected on time. These feelings cause a lot of physical diseases and mental anguish to humans and can cause their lives to go downhill fast, inviting to themselves all the bad lucks and in extreme could cause them to hurt others literally as to commit crimes.

Every human being had experienced all these emotions in some ways sometime in his life and it is okay if we can get out of these emotions on time or before they can harm us or harm other people.

There is only one effective virtue that can heal us from all these diseases of the soul and it is FORGIVING.

Here I am going to present one method of forgiving that can effectively clear our soul from all these painful emotions. But before I do that, I would like to share some experience of a haunting feeling of being betrayed or lied on by the most important person in my life at the time.

My father was the most important person in my life especially when I was in my teen, fifteen years old to be exact. It was in this age when my Dad pulled me out from my school in Davao City to be transferred back to Cagayan De Oro City to finish my high school. School for me was the most important place in my life at the time because I value Education and considered it to be my stepping stone for my future success. But in Cagayan De Oro City he did not enroll me to my previous school, instead he let me stay with our family in the farm. Once we were settled there, he left to a faraway place for his missionary work. He said nothing about my study. One month later he came home to us, it was a Friday and after our confrontations about my study he told me to prepare my luggage because he said that on Sunday we will be going to the city where I could continue with my study. I was so elated even when I knew that I would be late. I was singing and was very happy thinking and believing that I would be in school the following week. Then Sunday came I woke up early in the morning only to discover that my Dad had gone at dawn. My Mom said that my Dad won't be home for six months and that I should not expect to go back to school for this year or perhaps years and years after. His reason was that going to school is useless because "Jesus is coming very soon."

God how I hated my Dad at that time. The kind of hatred that caused me to disrespect him even in front of many people. That incident really changed me and my behavior a lot also changed my view about men, that men are liars and I can easily yell at them.

As a result of my Dad's betrayal and lie to me my

relationships with men became difficult and my energy would invite men who are liars and would cheat on me.

Years later in my introspections and questions why I can't find a man who is pure in all intentions I happened to read the book of Shakti Gawain which discussed about forgiving. Only then I realized that deep in me was a huge block to my happiness in my relationships with men especially in marriage.

Here I am going to share how to forgive first yourself and every person who had hurt your feelings from the past or even at present.

Of all the most abused person we come across that hurt us constantly or who we hurt constantly is ourselves. I used to say to myself "You're a fool Senotiza," every time I realized I made a wrong decision. This statement is hurting our souls in the deep level. Do you say I am crazy? I am foolish? I am lazy? I am ugly? I am a dunce? Or any other demeaning terms to yourself every time you make mistake or do something wrong? We may just take for granted what we are saying to ourselves but our souls are listening and we become what we often say to ourselves carelessly. Therefore, it is important that we have to forgive ourselves by this affirmation. "I love, forgive, and accept myself completely as I am." Write this statement 30 times a day in 28 days.

We cannot forgive other people if we have not completely forgiven ourselves.

Once you are cleared and had completely forgiven yourself the next thing to do is to begin to forgive every other person who had hurt your feelings, start from the past or those people closest to you like your parents. In my case, it was my Dad.

It doesn't matter whether the person is dead or alive or that you will never see him again, just do the forgiving in the mental level and in ritual manners such as this. I wrote a letter to my Dad in this manner;

Dear Papa,

You really hurt me in the past, you hurt my feelings when you lied to me about my going back to school and you betrayed me by not keeping your promise to me. But I want to forgive you now to dissolve the block of energy in my system. I forgive you now Papa. Go your way as I go mine. God bless you.

This is the sequence of the forgiving format;

1. Address the person on his/her name.
2. Tell him which part of your person was being hurt, emotional? Physical, if he literally beat or kick you, etc.
3. State what he did to you that hurt you;
4. Express your desire to forgive;
5. Reason of forgiving is to dissolve this hurt feeling which block the flow of good energy in your system;
6. Then say I forgive you now. Go your way as I go mine.
7. Then bless the person by merely saying "God bless you."

After doing a lot of forgiving in this manner to people who I thought had hurt me, only then had my relationship with a man and even with my whole family became meaningful and harmonious.

The bottom-line is that, it is safe to say that to forgive ourselves and others in the deepest sense brings us not only happiness and peace but also all the blessings and good lucks into our lives. So what are you waiting for? FORGIVE NOW!!!!

22

THREE POWERFUL WORDS TO PONDER FOR A MEANINGFUL LIFE

Now the three words. First is "Remember" next is "Love" and last is "Faith". Here I will elaborate why these three words are so powerful especially when you are at the lowest point of your life.

First, I would like to remind here that problems are just lessons in life that we are going to face and tackle wisely. If problems seem so huge, whatever it maybe we have the power to turn them small and surmountable. It's in the mental attitude of the subject. If you think that your problem is huge and beyond your ability to solve and you feel like you want to run away from it, remember that it's your mental attitude towards a problem that make it monstrous so wherever you go it follows you and whatever you do will always result to becoming another problem and worse it gets bigger and bigger.

Given the precedent as right, we cannot run away from problems, we have to face them and dissolve them.

The question then is how do we dissolve problems in life? Answer is to use your inherent power that is just lying dormant within you. Use these three words that are so powerful to live by.

Remember... Remind yourself to remember who you are and what you are. Remember you are a precious soul in the eyes and heart of God. Remember that Jesus died for you. If you are not a Christian, remember that you are a part of this universe and you have something to contribute to the welfare of humanity. Remember your love for yourself, remember where you are good at. Remember those who love you. Remember your past achievements and what else you can do and become in the future. Remember how you were able to solve and surpassed past problems that you had encountered. Remember you are here in life because you are victorious, you are a winner. Remember that at the time of your conception there were millions of zygotes who raced towards being fertilized in your mother's egg to become human and you championed them all and most of all remember that problems resolve themselves and life supports itself. The bottom line is to remember all the good experiences and the beauty of life and living.

Love...The second powerful word is LOVE. First love yourself for being you including your faults and flaws. See in your mind's eye how lovable you are, how good you are in something. Then see in your mind's eye your loved ones, parents, children, spouse, lover, etc. scrutinize what make them so lovable. Also see in your mind's eye those beautiful things that you admire, possessing them and enjoying them, feel the joy of having them.

Faith...Last but not least, let faith do miracles in your situation now and your whole life. Have faith in the saying "This too will pass. "Problems resolve themselves." "God will take care of me" The point is to fill your mind with powerful statements and affirmations to inspire you to act positively to face your situation. Be honest to yourself and to every person that you are dealing with. If you are at fault accept your fault with humility. Forgive and apologize. Un burden yourself from any negative situations and trust that things will work out right for you.

23

ORGANIZE YOUR DREAMS

Can you remember the time when you started becoming aware of your mind creating dreams or fantasizing about things that you think you will enjoy doing, having or becoming? These activities of the mind are stronger and more frequent during puberty or teen years of our lives. It is also the period of our development when we get moodier and this is because our minds are full of imaginary things and cannot settle yet into something that we really want in our lives. This is the stage of development where many teenagers experience identity crisis of all sorts. There are anxieties about the future and we are easily affected positively or negatively by anything in our environment, by parents, siblings, family relationships as a whole and even with peer groups. Then with these confusing response to environment we tend to go back to our selves by dreaming and creating imaginary situation, locations and even characters that we feel comfortable and happy about.

There is nothing wrong in dreaming for as long as you are in control even in your dreams. Be careful of what you dream of because dreams do come true in ways you never know when and how.

The fact that thoughts are things and everything that is existing started in the mind of the creator should warn us to be aware of the contents of our minds. Are your dreams creative and constructive? or are they vindictive or destructive? Are your thoughts full of vengeful imaginations and anger? Do you notice that the contents of your mind affect your feelings? For example if you are angry with somebody who insulted you and you cannot keep your mind still when it seems to repeat the words that made you feel insulted then this thoughts will block you from creating beautiful dreams because you will be overcome with the feelings of anger. This is what I meant in my previous discussion as blocks to our creative energy.

Dreams do come true so be careful of what you dream of. Dreams come true and they manifest in the right sequence and in perfect timing. Very often as humans we want everything to happen as quickly as we had thought of it, this may be true in real life as the case may be but in terms of the layout of our lives, we are subject to time elements. We follow sequences and steps in our development. We cannot be adults first before we spend years being teen-agers. There may be some overlaps in behaviors and way of thinking depending on the culture and individual gene but just the same, we follow the stages in human development.

With this fact, we are controlled by time and stages of our lives, so are the sequences of our dreams. If you dream to be rich for example, dream first about what you want to become and what you do before you dream to be rich and how rich you want to be. There are three basic sequences of our dreams and they are as follow;

1. Dream on what you want to become; example, to be a doctor, a teacher, a businessman, and whatever it is that you want to become. See yourself in your mind's eyes how you look and behave when your dream about yourself comes true.

2. Dream on what you are doing as the person you become in the first step. If your dream is to be a doctor, see yourself doing surgery or diagnosing a disease of a patient and that you are clothed in white outfits as doctors do.

3. Dream about riches. In your mind's eye see yourself as a successful person in whatever you are doing and that your success brings you a lot of money, count them and see what you spend your money for, such as house and lot, cars, travels, whatever.

The bottom-line is that, to organize your dream is to dream according to the sequence of your development and you have to understand that those dreams that come true follow the sequence of our development. Dream wisely.

24

THE TYPES OF DREAM AND THE TYPES OF PERSONALITY THAT CAN MAKE A DREAM COME TRUE

There are many people who cannot dream, let alone seeing their dreams coming true if they do dream.

Not everybody is capable to create a real dream and those who cannot dream don't have directions in their lives, they are like rubbish thrown to the vast ocean, floating to where the wind blows them and floating with no concrete direction to land on.

Whereas a person who can dream correctly and clearly will have a vivid imagination of his future and the kind of life that he pursues then fills his mind with ideas and finding answers to his questions on how he can make his dream come true.

The types of dreams that can come true are those that deal with the personal wellbeing of the dreamer such as health, beauty, relationships socio-economic condition and status quo.

Many people attempt to create a dream but only few make their dreams come true. Those who fail to make their dream come true are the ones who has no patience and persistence. Patience and persistence are two valuable virtues of a dreamer. With these virtues nothing can come between the dreamer and the reality of his dreams, nothing can discourage him whatsoever. No amount of failures or discrepancies can stop him from pursuing his dreams, even if it would just be in his mind.

I will present my case here as an example. When I started dreaming to live in America, my first attempt to do it was to have an interview with the US embassy in the Philippines to get a tourist visa, I failed not once but thrice. Then I tried to find another way, I involved myself in pen pal writing where I thought I may be able to come over to America with an American spouse or fiancé. This attempt though was not acceptable in my moral values system because I was still married at that time so I had to leave my husband first so I will have freedom to find a new one, an American for that matter. The story will be very long if I will go through, the idea is just to prove that dreams do come true if you are serious about it. From the onset of this dream to live in America to the point of it coming true took me two and a half decades to materialize.

Like I said, dreams do come true but there are many various twists and turns along the way that includes changing your thought processes and Values system.

The whole idea is that, persistence, patience, determination, the ability to blend with any situation that come along and open-mindedness are the keys and personal powers of the dreamer that make his dream come true.

25

THE PHILOSOPHY BEHIND PERFECT TIMING

Perfect timing controls all the stages of development of life in all areas. All humans are controlled by time and space. Observe the human development from conception to the time of his passing away from this life. In between are a complex of adventures and misadventures. Even at the onset of conception is in itself a perfect timing. Among the millions of zygotes that raced towards the fertilized egg of the mother, you championed it because you got the perfect timing and was conceived while the rest were just wasted away. You became a human from then on and the journey in life began.

You started in complete dependence to your location, the womb. Your food intake, your blood, your breath, your comfort or discomfort were all dependent on your mother's womb in the material sense but above all that you didn't have to plan intentionally for what your life is going to be, there would be a perfect time for such a development. All human beings evolve into something. In this particular stage of development where everything that you are depends on your location, the womb and the mother, most importantly nature or the natural process of development as controlled by the time of your stay inside the womb, all you can do is to relax and wait mostly unconsciously(?) I put a question mark after the word "unconsciously" because there are new studies now that show that the fetus is aware of what is going on even outside the womb such as it hears the mother's voice and the people she socialize with even the noise and music around the mother.

It is compulsory for the fetus to come out from the womb in the perfect time, ceteris paribus, meaning everything in that pregnancy is normal. Perfect timing does not stop at birth. The next stage of development follow right after the baby is born. Many changes occur, the change of environment and everything different from where he had been for nine months, the food, relationships with people around, recognizing objects and sounds then acting on his likes and dislikes, the baby has to cope with all of these right after birth onward in his babyhood.

Life adventure is getting more complicated as the baby grows in years and physical changes. This reminds me of my eldest granddaughter when she was barely four years old. Her parents sent her to nursery school where they had to learn the alphabets and she had many assignments, mostly recognizing drawings, shapes and colors. One day my daughter's friend visited us carrying her one-year old toddler. My granddaughter played with him and I heard her say to the toddler "I envy you because you are care-free and have no problems" then I asked her, why, what are your problems? She answered, many school homework.

As we journey on in life, we pass through a lot of stages of requirements to fit with the socio-cultural norms of the society we are in. Learning and education are very important development to become a respectable and responsible person. And we have dreams for ourselves that require personal effort to achieve. Life has many twists and turns, many of them natural but there are always individual reasons and differences that we do something that our peers don't agree, worse contradict.

But then there is always a perfect time for everything in our individual lives. There is a perfect time to dream, a perfect time to accomplish or act on your dream, a perfect time to wait and relax because when your perfect time to succeed or achieve comes nothing can stop it. Your soul knows the perfect timing for you, it made it happen when you championed at the time of conception. You won the victory when among the millions who raced to the fertile egg of your mother you were the one honored to become human. Life is not a race for who would be the best person in anything because every human is a champion in his own right but life is a race for the perfect timing of your becoming the perfect person and personality that you can be. Consult your own soul for a truly victorious life.

26

HOW LONG DOES IT TAKE FOR A DREAM TO COME TRUE?

We humans are all subject to time and conditions in our environment or space; and not only that, we are also controlled by the gene, norms and other cultural aspects in such an environment. When a dream is born in a particular person, he normally wants such a dream to come true in an instant, otherwise he may lose interest in such a dream because many opposing thoughts could crop up into his mind in time before the dream materializes. He even does some trials and errors and is often discouraged when he meets some failures in his attempts and endeavors.

I would like to reiterate here that dreams do come true, sooner or later, we just have to be patient and to be emotionally disconnected or detached from it when the correct procedures of creating the dream has been done.

The journey from the onset of a dream or goal towards its manifestation or materialization is full of twists and turns, also bumps loopholes; some dreams manifest quickly and easily while others take years, even decades to come true. These all depend on how simple or sophisticated a dream is. It is always a good feeling to dream big but along with such big dream should come patience and discernment.

A dream normally begins in several situations such as the constant experience of deprivation, being attracted to experience better and beautiful objects or conditions in life and many others. A dream starts with a wish, a wish is just a wish you don't believe it can come true and you just let it pass. While it is true that some wishes do come true but in general wishes are just passing whims of the mind; those that come true may had been inside you for some time which suddenly comes back when triggered by some experience for the moment.

To make a dream come true you must work it out from the inside. First, acknowledge your wishes then choose which of these wishes is actually important to you. After deciding on the most important wish, create an affirmation to that writing it down in the correct affirmation format; first, second and third person. Do some more rituals by sketching, drawing or collecting pictures of that dream then paste your own picture beside it writing down your thoughts, for example if your dream is a foreigner or American husband. Cut out a picture of any American guy that is attractive to you then cut out a picture of you paste it beside the man's picture and write, this is me and my American husband beside me. Make a poster of that picture and post it on your wall...just post it and don't be too excited about it, detach yourself emotionally from that dream.

There would be twists and turns sometimes you will be

relocated to a place where you may meet unintentionally the person of your dream, sometimes it will be meeting that person unexpectedly. Don't ask yourself how you will meet because you might find a way to do it and it won't be effective, just detach yourself from thinking about it tell yourself that dreams do come true and the perfect time for it to happen will surely come.

Dreams that involve a little amount of money for your personal needs are quicker to come true if you know the perfect affirmation to it. Such statements as "My God shall supply all my needs according to his riches in glory" Money come to me easily and effortlessly in very satisfactory and harmonious ways," God is my source of supply meeting all my needs in perfect timing at all times." And more of these sorts make them the contents of your mind instead of worrying where and how you will get money for your needs.

The bottom line is dreams do come true, create them intentionally and correctly then program your mind to the faith that dreams do come true in perfect timing.

27

SUGGESTED LIST OF ACTIVITIES TO LIVE LIFE THE EASIER WAY

There is no absolute method to live life easily. Life is movement, like I always say, the direction is forward and development to progress. But then life is an adventure from the time of conception to the time life ends in this material world. As an adventure we encounter countless struggles in all forms that oftentimes put us in the crossroads of which way to take and many times too we choose the wrong road, but life is no turning back, life is controlled by time and space, we can change direction but which direction again to choose, if any? Being in the wrong direction in the first place is by itself already confusing how then can you change direction if turning back is not an option? How can you change the direction of your life if you cannot find another way out? So many people in this confusing life situation would surrender to their truth by saying "I have no choice" "I was born into a poor family therefore I should accept my fate in life." "There is nothing I can do to move on to a better life, I am deprived of all means, doors to opportunities are closed on me" and many more of these sorts.

The truth is, there's more to life than what you are seeing and hearing in your immediate environment.

Following are suggestions of what to do in whatever life situation that is trapping you:

1. Dare to dream the impossible. If you think it is impossible for you to go to school and finish a degree then dream it. If you think it is impossible for you to live a life having everything you need for comfort and luxury, then don't worry...it is impossible for you? Then dream it, to dream is possible, right?

2. Affirm your dreams regularly through writing and spoken words.

3. When a wonderful idea comes up in your mind write them down and do it immediately.

4. Stop complaining about your difficult situation, look at the beauty and brighter side of life and let them be the contents of your mind regularly and permanently.

5. When negative thoughts try to invade your mind and feelings, think and say the opposite; for example, if your thoughts say "it's impossible for me to get out from my very poor condition in life" say the opposite "it's possible and easy for me to live a rich and beautiful life." If your mind says "it's impossible for me to find the man who can truly love me" say the opposite "my perfect match come to me easily and effortlessly" and so forth and so on depending on the specific situation that you are in...just say the

opposite of that dilemma that trap you, the mind works in opposites.

Remember that life is an adventure of twists and turns and one has to deal each of these with the power that is inherent in every living human. Wise people deal every situation in their lives using their personal power and strength so that their efforts emanate from within.

28

RE-INVENTING YOUR
SELF AND YOUR LIFE

It is very easy to say "stop doing those things you used to do if you want a result different from what you are experiencing now."

Re-inventing your self is the most tedious if not complex thing to do so why bother?

Check out your life in these terms; health, beauty, fashion, house/home, relationships/romance/family/peer groups/social and corporate positions/status quo, career, money, hobbies/fun/leisure/sports/travels/handicrafts, mobility, material possessions/car, gadgets/property and assets, education and specific knowledge acquisition/ spirituality, the list could go on but for the purpose of listing what could be valuable to keep life a real haven of joy we will just be contented in this list. I will discuss each of these items in the list thoroughly with the objective to diagnose in the individual level the defects if any that needs improvement or re-invention and to prescribe the methods leading to the desired results.

Re-inventing your Health patterns

As you notice, health is always top in the list for obvious reasons. Health is freedom from chronic pain, freedom to do anything that requires strength and physical efforts and be able to be anywhere you want and to do anything to enjoy life. Health is also shown in the glow of the skin, the twinkle in the eyes, the laughter and all the enthusiasm that a person demonstrates. In this definition of health, you notice that health is an index to the emotional and spiritual condition of an individual hence, it's safe to say that a healthy person is a happy person that lives life to the fullest. There is no excuse, if your life misses the standard of being healthy then there is something for you to do, to re-invent yourself in order to get that kind of health described here. Is it possible for you? Just say yes and let your psyche agree with that yes and everything will be possible for you.

You will notice in our later discussion as we go along that most, if not all the prescription to re-invent any or all of the defects in described here will be to redirect the pattern that your psyche had created for you and for your lifetime to follow.

Still on health, what have you discovered about your health? Have you experienced something like you cannot eat a certain type of food because you are convinced that it will make you sick and that you had actually got sick when you tried to eat it and more so, your doctor had told you not to eat such a food for your health's sake? In this situation, your psyche had bought into the idea that you get sick if you eat such a food. Let's have this scenario such that the easiest food for you to get is that food that will make you sick, will you starve yourself to death? You will die in the belief that had been accepted by your psyche and had created a pattern to punish you if you divert?

This is just an example but let's follow the trend. Try to re-invent yourself and go straight to your psyche, tell it that you are now redirecting its pattern of belief that you now allow yourself to eat the food and won't be punished by getting sick. Remember that you are higher than the beliefs this world can influence you, change the pattern of belief that your psyche had made for you, even the patterns of belief were created by you through experience and outside influences.

Once you had successfully redirected the belief pattern in your psyche you will see the re-invented you in this particular situation. You will notice that your fear of eating such a food had banished and that you eat the food without any hesitation and you don't get sick. See? A simple re-invention of yourself, just work it from the real you, the soul in you.

You can go on to self-diagnose yourself in this health issues that prevent you from enjoying life. Such issues in health as obesity, exercises, food, medications etc., see how they affect you and your belief systems that need to be changed or redirected. Ask yourself the questions, did I just hear them and had bought into their reality? What does my body and situation really need and can afford?

This method is applicable in all areas of your life just use it for your own good and for the good of all concerned.

29

GOD: RELIGION AND OPEN-MINDEDNESS-

There is learning and wisdom in having an open mind to anything presented in the universe. I will discuss here open-mindedness in terms of God and religion. I do believe in God if God is defined as the Force and the Greatest Intelligence or the Power that keep things going in this universe including the tiniest thing that exists here and most importantly including, we humans.

If you have an open mind you won't easily be get carried away by religious groups that define to you what God can do for you because you already know and what you know about God is your own experience with Him. You as a human being are made to make mistakes and to learn from your mistakes, learning from your mistakes is a process in which eventually you learn to formulate strategies that is uniquely applicable to only you. In the process of learning, you learn to call on a Higher power to help you achieve what you really want in life and what you really want to achieve; such power is something you personally believe works for you and if you believe then whatever you believe is done unto you, this is the law of nature. Having an open mind will cause you to develop in your own personal phase of development. You will develop self-awareness, you also develop being aware of others, their nature and their needs so you offer help when needed. You have a self-sufficient mind that knows where you had been, where you are now and where you are going. You know exactly what you are, what you want and what to do for the achievement of your goals. You don't allow any person to intervene with your personal affairs because they know nothing about you, about your desires, about your faith and trust in the universal power that had been guiding you all the way; it's between you and your God. You don't need to be exploited by religious leaders and belonging to a group of the same religion people in order to become an achiever or a self-actualized human. You just need you and God and the playground of God where you are now, the universe and the laws in it that govern it.

You don't compete with others especially in terms of righteousness because you understand the natural law of variation. You know that what works for you may not work for others because each is made different even in understanding, perception and response to any given stimulus at a time. You won't impose to others what you truly believe in, you may share your knowledge and probably teach if needed and asked but never impose; you have a very wide range of tolerance and you allow anyone to be them, to be what they are. You are not judgmental which is the problem with many so-called religious leaders, they disobey what they teach, they may have read Matthew 7: which says "Judge not that ye may not be judged. For whatever mete you measure to someone will be measured back to you" You know that if one breaks the natural laws, he himself will suffer the consequences of his own actions and you can only learn from other people's mistakes too but never condemn. One of the many advantages of having an open mind is that you naturally avoid stress in life. You don't compete, jealousy, envy and hatred have no place in your heart because you understand that this is a rich universe and everybody has a fair share of what is good here. You see only the good sides of life. This does not mean though that you are not aware of the darkness but you don't focus yourself to the darkness, the only way to banish darkness is to shine and since you shine the darkness just fades naturally.

The bottom line here is that your religion cannot give you a good life, it just limits you from being you and from doing those things that could have given you a life that is beautiful, a life that reflects the beauty that is God. Godliness is not measured by any degree of adherence to any religious teachings.

30

JUST FEEL IT... FEEL AND LIVE IT

Embrace life, feel it, and live it.

Feel beautiful, don't think you are beautiful because you will just hear within you some negative reactions, just feel beautiful then embrace yourself and say "I love you (whisper your name), you are so beautiful!"

Feel blessed or lucky, don't think you are lucky because you will just be reminded of all the heartaches and failures in the past and of all your defects and flaws...thinking is a torture, feeling is good. Count your blessings and say aloud "I am lucky, I am blessed, I am a winner! "The fact is there are failures and successes in life, drop the failures they are just parts of the lessons in life that catapult you to the next level. The fact that you are still alive in this stage of your life only means that you have more successes than failures so congratulate yourself, Celebrate! Feel it!

Feel rich, don't think you are rich because it will just remind you of your debts and your empty wallet. Again, rationalizing your financial condition just gives you headaches and tantrums. Feel you are rich, as rich as the Universe, as abundant as the water in the ocean and as the leaves of the trees and as the sand in the beach. Be awed by the abundance of everything in nature in which you are nature yourself, not just a part of nature but the crown of all creation! Be awed by its abundance and say to yourself "Yes! I am rich! I am abundance! Feel it and live your daily life with this feeling in your heart.

Emotions are the transportation that you ride in this life. Emotions take you to your destiny but you are the driver. Drive your emotions to the right direction, to the direction that your heart desires to reach. Discard rationalization if they just block you from your destination in life. Thinking is good only if they obey your desires. Thinking too much is limiting your ability, it paralyzes your capability because thinking is not originally yours, you just pick them from anybody, anywhere and anything that surround you in any given moment and stage of your life and they accuse you of being poor, inadequate, ugly and unlucky and sickly among other painful thoughts. Stop rationalizing. Just feel your desire and it will take you there...there in your life's true destiny.

Life is difficult you think? Discard the thought and feel the abundance, go to the beach and behold the abundance of the water in the sea and the ocean, go to your garden and count the leaves of the flowers, the trees and the grasses, can you count them? or count the strands of hair on your head, even when you are balding there are still strands of tiny hair around your head...Feel the wonders of abundance in the universe, you are that...Just feel it. It's your choice. What you feel is what you become and your life would be.

Part II

Part 2 of this book are excerpts from my first book entitled Spice Up Your Soul. I collected some of them especially the poems that express some important times of our lives.

1

LIFE CYCLES AND PATTERNS

When my Kiwi husband Adrian was still alive, we had an Italian friend called Joe, one day he asked me "Jenny, if you were to go back to your childhood, will you do the same things, the same mistakes that you had done in your life?" I was not prepared for this question so I said, you initiated the idea for such a question, answer it yourself. Then he said "I am still me basically so I would still do the same mistakes and the same things."

Given the premise that an individual life develops based on inherited genes and nurture, it is understandable that a certain individual will repeat everything that he has done including mistakes because he is just following the threads and webs of the pattern that his psyche had created for him. The pattern is imprinted in the psyche or the soul that governs the perception and behaviors of an individual in a given situation and stimulus.

I had been watching on TV and YouTube these women behind bars, particularly those sentenced for life without the possibility of parole. A great percentage of these women, say 80% who are mothers would cry and would express regrets for what they had done that led to their present destination. They had put an end to the real enjoyment of life, they lost their right to their children and become undeserving mothers so that their children are given away for adoption. Their marriage is broken and their husbands has to move on with a new wife. Their basic freedom is gone, they have to obey the rules in the prison.

There was this particular woman who caught my attention. She is presently 56 years old and had been in and out of prison five times in the past and this is her sixth and final destination, she will stay in prison till she dies there. Her first offense was DUI (driving under the influence), she got short jail time...next offense was drug use and dealings, the jail time had increased, her next offense was brutal attack and public obstruction of peace, the jail time increase the more, next offense was armed robbery to support her drug addiction, and the latest that put her to jail for life is murder, homicide.

If you notice, the cycle is a spiral movement, the cycle has increased its intensity and going up to a higher and higher level every time. Once you start one wrong decision in your life, your psyche would take note of it and will create a pattern that you follow in every given similar situation. This woman was crying in the interview, she has children and grandchildren and regrets that she cannot enjoy their presence like any normal mothers and grandmothers do. She seems to regret what she has done, but does she really? She had five chances to discard her ways of violence but she just spiraled to worse and worst activities every time she had the chance.

This type of women has inherent weaknesses of

characters, they only see dark sides of life and would create and do another darkness because they have something to blame on and as they do, the psyche creates the pattern and they cannot get out of it anymore.

Whereas, say if you have started your life right such as instead of drinking alcohol when problems come you ask yourself or psyche what is the best thing to do given the situation, in this sense your psyche will create a pattern of finding solutions for you whenever you are in a conflicting situation. You can trust your psyche, your true self to do what is only best for you.

The question then would be, "What if I had done a lot of wrong things in my life and my psyche had already created a pattern for those wrong decisions, can I correct the pattern?" The pattern will stay as it is, it cannot be corrected but you can divert or re-invent a pattern by telling yourself, your psyche that you are diverting or reinventing yourself and your life and you have to consult it every time to plan for your future or face a difficult situation. Once you and your psyche had developed that kind of agreement then you are in the right path to re-inventing yourself and your life as a whole.

2

A BEAUTIFUL LIFE

Look at a variety of flowers in a garden, they differ in species, colors, sizes and forms but they are beautiful. Just like life each of us have different paths and destiny to follow but the fact that we live on is a beauty by itself. Roses are beautiful, tulips too as well as gladiolas and the rest of the species of flowers but they don't look the same, each of these species have beauty peculiar to each of them. Think of life this way, you don't compare your life to the life of your friend or anybody else, your life is yours and its beautiful.

Can you say that your life is beautiful? I had been talking to many friend pasts and present, some would say they are happy with their lives now but most of them would discuss only on difficulties. The fact is difficulties or abundance, life is still beautiful. Embrace life including everything that is in it. In sorrow, in pain, in difficulty or in good luck and abundance, they are there to make life colorful and beautiful. If your life is all red, meaning abundant in material things, and red only devoid of any other color then you will get bored very soon. Difficulties are there for us to use our inherent creative minds and as reminders to call on the power greater than ours, human.

Can you still say life is beautiful if your spouse leaves you for another, or if romantic love had jumped out the window for good?

I know the miserable feelings of this situation no matter what the reason. To have a broken heart is among the worst experiences you will ever have. The feelings of being betrayed, abandoned followed by feelings of being not beautiful or attractive enough to keep your lover stick with you and all the rest of self-pity and self-inadequacies that could lead to 0 self-esteem and self-hate. Many people would commit suicide as a result of a broken heart or broken marriage or of being jilted by a lover, others still will lose self-control and would kill. Being betrayed by a lover is one of the most bitter and powerful emotional states that could happen to people. Now going back to my question, can you still say that life is beautiful in this situation? The answer is "it's in the mind". Your mind is more powerful than your most powerful emotion. It's the mind that dictates emotion. Weigh everything in the balance. Do some "advantage-disadvantage" analysis. Write down the negative-positive aspects of your relationship, enumerate the pain he caused you and the advantages of his absence in your life. The bottom line is you have to be always for you. Don't allow one person to discredit the beautiful you. You don't lose him/her...he/she is the loser to have lost you. Tell yourself you are a wonderful person, list down what makes you wonderful no matter what and he/she lost that wonderful person in his/her life. Do not punish yourself with nonsense self-pity and feelings of inadequacy. You are the one who makes your life beautiful...I know it's easier said than done but just do it; make your life beautiful, remember you are the creator of your own life and destiny.

Can you still say life is beautiful even when you are broke, buried in debts and the creditors are after you, hungry, cannot feed yourself and your family and jobless with no source of income?

These are survival needs. The answer is still in the state of mind. Remember those times when you had everything, a good job, a good income and so forth. There has to be some reasons that lead to this situation of your life. Perhaps you were fired from your job because you ran short of insight to keep it or perhaps you left your job because you were sick or maybe you had to run away from the place where your last job was because of a broken marriage; in this case this is a double misery but it's not the end of the world. Tell yourself "Problems resolve themselves and life supports itself". Think of the birds, the fish and everything in nature, they survive naturally so do you. List down all your abilities and those things you really love doing and see yourself doing them and earning money from them. See yourself as being able to pay your bills and your debts. It's in the mind. Instead of wallowing in the miserable state of mind let your mind lift you up to a place where you can do everything you want and, in a situation, where you can be everything you want to be. At the same time, face your creditors and accept the punishment or consequences of your delinquency with the mind that one day you will get out from the situation you are in the present. The bottom line is the principle "this too will pass". Nothing is permanent in life. Money come and go, people come and go, difficulties come and go, just look forward to the perfect timing that you can live your life according to your desires.

Remember life is beautiful because you can make it beautiful. You are the artist of your own life and being an artist, you can choose beauty to put into your canvas.

3

COME HOME TO ME

Emotions, desires, yearnings and all the longings of the heart are evidences of being alive. The following poem is an expression of a yearning heart. The idea is you have to acknowledge your feelings in every given moment of your life and express them in a manner that will make you feel better, after all you are the only person who knows yourself fully in every second of your life. Loneliness will be eased if you take care of your feelings all the way.

Here it goes...

Come Home to Me

You are my thoughts as I fall asleep at night;

The solitary hero in my dreams as I am deeply asleep through the darkest dawn;

You are my first recall when I awake in the first glimpse of the rising sun.

My longing heart awaits your re-appearance;

Praying for the day when you finally come home to stay;

You've been wandering too long and too far away from me;

For you have long forgotten the warmth of my loving arms.

Deep in my soul is the sweetest remembrance of you;

The memory of us together embeds itself to the fabric of my essence;

In my Utopia I search for you; Calling your name let us revive our love anew.

If perchance you opt to desert me for good; Please let me know of your intention;

I can forgive your choice of omission but remembrance of you is my sole consolation.

Decades and centuries are mere fragments of time;

My immortal soul may wander through the gloom;

But I will come home at any clime and season;

Still hoping and remembering that we were both here together once upon a time.

4

A POETIC NARRATIVE: HALFWAY TO MY DESTINY

The following is a narrative poem that symbolizes the twists and turns of life.

Destiny

Halfway to My Destiny:
In the heat of the noontime sun here I stand;
Amidst the debris of my shattered sanctuary;
Sweating, trembling, weary, hungry and thirsty;
From such fearful and horrible experience,
Yet I am just halfway towards the end of this very long day.
If I may recall how this day had started;
From the darkest dawn in a faraway place of my origin;
I was awakened by the terrifying howling of the unknown.

I should have preferred to go back to sleep to be cradled in darkness, if there was an assurance of safety and peace.

The breaking of the day brought instant hope to me; I thought of starting the day right for a long journey;

I knew that I had to be rooted out from my birthplace; But where to, I didn't know.

Then I slowly made a step away from such confusing sight; Trailing the pathway before me; hoping to end towards a brighter destiny.

Such hope though had quickly faded when along the trail I met this hermit, Indicating that I must be in the wilderness;

Hence, I resolved to hold on to courage and inner strength;

If I wished to survive and get out from this place. The old man told me of my location; That I was in a danger zone; then he led me to a crossed pathway;

And said he cannot escort me farther; He left me to decide which path to follow;

Then warned me to prepare myself; For whatever consequences my choice may lead.

I trod alone on the pathway that I had chosen when the old wiz had long been gone;

The heat of the brightening sunlight had now started to bite my skin;

While my feet ached as I continued to walk on;

Thorns and thistles abound along the bushes as I progressed;

Regrets haunted my mind for this difficult path I had chosen; But how could I know that the path I had not chosen was better than this?

Besides, to turn back now is too late.

When at the end of this path I had chosen; I realized

that it was not after all too bad; for I was approaching a big beautiful tavern; And thought to myself that in this place I will establish an abode for my own. I thought that after all I am in fact among the luckiest travelers; When in the gateway a good-looking and cheerful host welcomed me. He told me that everything I needed was here and will all be given to me freely.

Such a beautiful and furnished abode for weary travelers like me;

Food, drinks, and comfort; bounties and kindness were too good to be true; He further said, "You can stay here for free and through eternity. Later in the tavern, which was actually a villa in the middle of nowhere; I was full and refreshed and ready to rest in the sleeping chamber assigned to me.

Suddenly a deafening and horrible growl outside the bedroom shocked me;

I ran towards the door and peeped in the keyhole; And there I saw the shadow of a huge and monstrous creature devouring bloody human beings; My reflexes instantaneously catapulted me and out through the back window I fled;

Ran, ran, ran as fast and as far away as I can for dear life; I continued to run until my muscles and my breath couldn't carry me farther; Was it an hour? Two hours of running? I ran through eternity till I collapsed and was breathless.

I must have fallen asleep for quite some time;

For when I came to, a lone horse rider was carrying me and set me on the horse back to ride;

I was still in a mentally disorganized state but my mind

was asking; Can my life be preserved? Do I have other choices?

Riding on horseback with him while I sleep along the way; And to a faraway city he took me;

Once in that city he said to me "In this city you can stay." But in my mind, I said "...a City of Fallen Angels..." It was a huge old castle but there never was an inhabitant; no not a soul.

In the castle we enjoyed the banquet on a long table; There was a cornucopia of all variety of food, dishes, fruit... I sat at the other end of that long table opposite him; With a queenly robe and a crown on my head, I was treated like a perfect queen;

If this was a dream then I wanted to sleep in my lifetime; Living the life of opulence and a king to take care of me.

His jolly mood and charming ways were contagious in the onset;

But in an instant, he turned into an ogre;

He thundered and roared like a howling wolf;

His devilish countenance expressed a vicious anger;

His eyes were red and blood ooze from it like tears; He picked a spear from out of the blue and cast it aimed towards my forehead;

But what he did not know; I saw what he would do while he was just thinking of it; And so, my trustworthy reflexes catapulted me once again from such a Devil's den.

As soon as I was safe and out of his reach; I cast away my crown and tore off my robe; for all of these are symbols of illusions and perfidy; I was almost completely naked when at the corner of my eyes I saw his shadow approaching me;

My first reaction was to run away as I always did in this situation; But I thought better and face him square instead;

Enough with running away; I die if I will, I have to face my enemy;

And so, with the loudest and most authoritative voice I can muster I thundered. "You are unreal! You are just a shadow! You are just a figment of my thought! A fruit of a weary mind!" And furthermore… "I am your Master! I am in control of my own destiny!"

Those powerful words that I uttered turned him instantly into an old limping hermit;

He was the one I met at the onset of my journey;

He suddenly stumbled and mumbled incorrigibly;

And withered like a dead tree before he finally burned to ashes.

As I turned my eyes to look where the castle stood; A huge and thick fog encompassed it;

And so, I ran towards it to see what had transpired; But when the fog cleared; what I saw was a gigantic pile of debris.

I turned again and raised my hands up high as I looked up the sky; And as I did, I felt a creeping miraculous strength tingling within me;

A refreshed feeling of victory and hope started to warm my body.

A realization warmed my blood as I learned of my life's designation; I realized that my destiny is actually just within me; my own strength and courage;

I am still halfway of this very long day; But I am revived and my strength is as the morn; And I still have enough time to build a home of my own.

Right here where I stand; Are valuable fragments of the castle that used to be here; I can gather those useful and valuable pieces;

Mend them and reshape them according to my wishes; From them I can recycle and build my own castle according to my own design;

The days of running and stumbling into strangers in unknown lands; Are now a thing in the past;

For where I stand is where my home of beauty, peace, love and abundance.

5

YOU ARE A WINNER

For those who sometimes, if not often feel that they had not done anything in their lives that they can be proud of, this article is for you. Remember that even in the womb of your mother there were millions of zygotes that raced to the egg of your mother's fertile egg to become a human eventually, you are the one who made it. That knowledge of this fact alone is a reminder that you are a winner.

Life has many challenges even at the onset but you had grown this far and you are still alive, perhaps sometimes happy and at times sad but you continue to live to experience more that life can offer. You had learned to walk, talk and everything there is to learn in your early stage of development in your own pace. You had gone to school to learn your ABC's both in reading and writing. Your mind had developed an understanding of those taught to you in school so that you had passed from one grade to the next and one level to another. Then you discovered later as you grow older that there are problems to be solved not only in school but also at home. You noticed the relationships at home with siblings and your parents. You also experienced sadness and happiness and learned what make you happy or sad.

You handle all your situations most often by yourself. It may be true that there are situations in your life where your parents and other people can help you out but most often it's you yourself has the final say when it comes to your feelings and convictions in a particular situation. Remember that there is nothing in life that can put you down if you won't allow it. Reminding yourself how you got out of trouble and solved your problems in the past will help you not only to survive but most important is to get what you what in life and to be successful, just as you had succeeded to become a human being even when you were still in the womb of your mother and the steps you had undergone to become the person that you are now. The winner, the achiever, the successful.

6

ACTIVITIES HUMAN BEINGS DO IN A LIFETIME

From birth to the end there are at least eight areas in life that keep people busy while still alive. Success in each of these areas would mean a lifetime of happiness and fulfillment. There should be a balance of success in every area because one area of life unattended will drag everything down and will eventually lead to a miserable life. On the other hand, too much concentration to just one area hence leaving everything else behind is as destructive to life. What are these areas? First let us trace our activities since birth and see if what we do are our own choice or are just dictated to us by society that includes our parents, religion, educators and everyone else involved. Let's try to recall what you did as a little child; who do you remember first, what did you do, what did you eat and so forth.

Human beings are made to be needy for a very good reason. Being in need makes one creative and productive hence would develop to be strong physically, spiritually and emotionally or as a complete human being. Unlike many lower forms of animals in the animal kingdom, human beings need to be taken care of and be nurtured 24 hours a day at birth till the baby learns the basic of independence in most areas in life, this takes around 2 years in average. During this time there is always the mother or the nanny to attend to all his needs, all the baby has to do is cry or scream and his needs are supplied. This human behavior very often causes a baby to enjoy too much that stage of development that psychologically he doesn't want to outgrow this comfortable stage.

While growth and mobility is the nature of life but along with it is the pain and the struggles. Once your life has started even as early as the time of conception in the womb of your mother the process of growth has also started and had been working for a definite period. At the time of birth, the infant cries because it had been very comfortably floating in the womb. The warmth, the comfortable darkness that keep him asleep and relaxed all the time, the softness of the "water bed" in the mother's womb are now replaced with glaring light, tough touch of the doctor, tough bed and some unexplained physical touch or sounds and the infant now feels some kind of need like hunger that he never felt while in the womb because it has been naturally supplied through its connection to its mother for nourishment. No matter how uncomfortable growth or birth is nothing could be done against nature. Each life has a time table. Nine months in the womb, 2 years for complete dependence to others in the basic needs, then what is next? There is always a perfect time for every stage of development in all areas of life and these are the major things that I am going to discuss after this introductory article under "Man's Activities in a Lifetime."

7

MAN'S ACTIVITIES IN A LIFETIME 2- THE FORMATIVE STAGE, 2 TO 6 YEARS OLD

We now continue our discussion on human development in all areas. Man is a complex being. To start with, during conception the fetus carries within him the genes of his parents and even the genes of his parents' parents up to five ancestral generations and even beyond as far as spirituality and other intangible components of his being is concerned. At the time of birth and early growth and development particularly when he had learned to be independent in basic self-service activities, his judgment or choices on how to do things are influenced by what he learned from his mother or nanny and his decision on whether he would do things to please his mother or he would do things because that pleases himself. Hence there's no such thing as all humans are equal completely, maybe equal in certain things but in everything, we are not. Some humans are rich, some are more intelligent, some are professionals, some are ugly, some are very attractive and so forth. Personality development comes in as the distinguishing factor in all of human endeavors. As the child grow, he would start to learn about many things. He would start to discover his preferences of food, like which one is delicious to his taste, he would also discover what kind of clothes is comfortable for him to wear, what color of clothes would attract him, he would also learn to acknowledge forms, sizes and colors. These are all-natural tendencies that a human would undergo but all these also would depend on a child's inherent nature. Some babies or toddlers don't care about anything but many children would already show repulsive behaviors about those things they don't like. This is how individuals differ, the personality and the culture will now come in. The earlier the child realizes or acknowledges his preferences in so many things in his surroundings and environment the earlier also will he know his needs and likes and once this happens, he will know what choices and alternatives he will have to get what he wants. People get what they want in various means. From crying and screaming to get what they want in the early stage he will learn later that this behavior won't work anymore as he grows older, he has to work his way out to get what he wants for example if he is thirsty he would go to the refrigerator or get the water to drink especially when nobody is around. The sense of independence will lead him to self-service and to figure out how he is going to meet his needs. In this stage, a child would learn that it's not just physical needs that he would meet. Approval from the parents and the people around him will be pleasing to him especially when there is encouragement from other people surrounding him. When the mother would appreciate what he does then he will always do things to please his mother.

And if the mother pampers him with demonstrations of love such as encouraging words, hugs and kisses the child learns to be loving too and would also learn to get what he wants through being lovable and loving. In short, the child will learn values formation at this early stage, he would begin to understand what is important to him and that is what he would need and desire to have in his life. This is the most important stage in a person's life. This is the formative years, what one learns to value in this stage will develop in spiral through his adult life.

8

Man's Activities in a Lifetime 3- The Peer Group Stage 6 to12 Years Old

This is the stage where a child becomes aware in a more serious way the importance in learning. He will learn many things outside of himself. Where prior to this stage he was more self-centered, this stage will make him realize that there are other children who are also important people in his surroundings. He will learn to socialize with other children and depending on his personality and perception he will learn to go along, to lead or to lag behind. This is the time for him to dream on what he wants as far as his relationship with other children is concerned. He will also learn to hero-worship, he will have many choices and interests aside from his lessons, if he has a high IQ and he knows how to use it for his popularity he will use it by studying seriously and be on the top of his class. He will discover many things about himself, he will discover where he is good at if only to be appreciated by his fellow children and his teachers.

His peer group relationship will also depend on his

formative years. If in his formative years he was convinced that he is lovable and loving and was always appreciated by his mother and other loved ones around the he will also do well in his peer group stage. He will be liked by everybody and even by his teachers, but even if many will like him there would still be some who would be jealous of him and would envy his achievements and position so he would also learn how to deal with such personalities. This is the stage where fighting is common among children as in physical fighting because children are sensitive to name-calling or labeling. In this stage a child will learn that there good and bad things, deeds and people that he has to deal with and can choose which way he should go. His ability to choose will have its function this time. Some would even would go to the extent where they have developed a strong liking to the beauty and other attractive qualities of the opposite sex; they will have crushes and would realize the strong feelings. Other children, especially those who have financial difficulty at home and whose parents always fight about money matters will develop attraction to those they believe to be rich based on their personal definition of being rich, the behavior would either be negative or positive, in the negative they will envy or get jealous of the rich child therefore would fight with him or he would invite others to be his allies to bully the better child; whereas in the positive, he will develop a strong desire to be rich someday and would start to dream on what he will do or would become when he grows up so that he can also get rich. The peer group stage is the starting point where desires and the sense of being needy by way of comparison to other children will open its door to the mind and character of an individual child.

9

MAN'S ACTIVITY IN A LIFETIME 4-PUBERTY

This is the stage where a person is in chaotic confusion with his being. He is not a child anymore and yet he is also not an adult. This is the transition and the crossroad that one should make a good choice in order to cross smoothly through a good life. Whatever one does and decides to do in this stage will determine the kind of life he would live throughout his remaining lifetime but it has also to be acknowledged that how one was brought up in his formative years and what he mostly value and give importance in his peer group years also determine his decision-making ability in this stage.

In this stage a person experiences a lot of physical changes including the voice as the voice changes according to the physical size of the larynx. Physical changes are very noticeable more particularly with the girls. Many teen age people cannot readily accept or get accustomed to these changes which means they feel awkward not only in their movement but also in their emotional state especially when they feel ugly like an "ugly duckling." This stage is mostly determined too by genetic component where some young people will start to bloom like flowers in spring, they would look very attractive to the point that some would marry this young. They are physically marriageable but most would make mistakes when they do marry this young because emotionally and spiritually, they are still immature to face the next stages of development especially in parenthood and financial aspects of life. As I said, there is a timetable in the process of development, just like the fetus in the womb, it should come out in perfect timing, if it comes out earlier than nine months there would be bad consequences, sometimes fatal and it cannot also overstay, the consequence would be bad for both mother and the fetus. Marriage is another development stage that should follow the timetable of development, there has to be a balance development in all three aspects, the physical strength, emotional stability, and spiritual power to face all the hurdles in life otherwise future destructive consequences would be more difficult to tackle.

Just like a pregnant woman, the time for the baby to be born does not depend on the size of the mother's stomach nor the size of the fetus in the womb. The fetus comes out based on the allotted time for it to be born.

Life is a journey or a development that is set by time, if you run too fast you will stumble and would cause yourself many bruises literally and symbolically; on the other hand if you run too slow you will be left behind and nobody will be with you when you need some helping hands in any areas of your situation, you will have a lot of backlogs, a lot of things undone and you will be lost and be frustrated in life.

This stage of puberty is the time for the individual to

scrutinize his dreams for himself making his dreams the dominating thoughts and seeing in his mind's eye what he would become in the future, the future that is set by time say five years or ten years from now. Then seeing himself living his life and working towards that direction. If he is sincere in making his life beautiful, he cannot be distracted by temporary beauty surrounding him if it won't contribute to his dream life for himself. His behaviors in any given situation are strongly influenced by his thought processes and mental attitudes which are in turn influenced by his upbringing in the previous stage of development.

10

A LIFETIME JOURNEY

The time of conception marks the beginning of a lifetime journey. The first stage of development begins in the womb where as we all know, it's all complete dependence from physical to emotional and spiritual. The next stage of the journey is the time the baby comes out from the womb up to seven years old, in average where the child learns the basics of taking care of his personal needs such as using spoons to feed himself, the toilet and such things as changing his clothes, perhaps more depending on the family status.

The journey continues on and on with so many adventures involving relationships. Relationship with himself, with objects around him, with animals, with plants with people and with nature or God and his creations.

In this lifetime journey we meet so many challenges and struggles that if taken wisely we will continue to be victorious in life just as we started to be victorious during conception. Every human being alive is meant to continue living a victorious life. Failure is for those who did not make it into human. The so-called failures in life are actually just lessons to be learned and to encourage humans to use their creative and analytic abilities.

A lifetime journey is filled with colorful experiences and challenging adventures.

11

LIFE IS MOVEMENT

Everything in life is movement, upward, downward, backward, forward, side-wards and in all directions in various speeds and phases of development. Everyone evolves in all areas of our lives, physical, emotional, spiritual, and knowledge-wise. Some of the areas in our lives just move on whether we like it or not. To cite one example, physical growth is inevitable for anyone born or that started as a baby or a newborn, whether in the animal kingdom or the plant kingdom. Change and evolution is a way of life, but then as responsible humans we take charge on nurturing our personal being in order to evolve into somebody who is an asset of society and to achieve the purpose of one's individual life. We have to pay attention to our physical health by taking the right food and physical activities for a balance and healthy physical growth; we also have to feed our minds with useful knowledge that we can use as a tool or tools to make our socioeconomic life meaningful, not only for ourselves but also for the good of everyone concerned. Most of all we have to nourish our spiritual life because it is the vehicle that transports us from one condition or situation to the next level in the process of our personal evolution. Growth, development, change and progress are evidences of a fulfilling life. In every person's heart and mind there is a vacuum that needs to be filled. We humans are born complete with potentials to achieve but we all need to discover what it is that we want to achieve in order to become a blessing in this life, mainly to ourselves then to our loved ones and to all concerned. To satisfy this painful longing in the soul, people resort to various behaviors and activities that he considers as the best way for him to do and achieve. The process of development is actually the path of happiness. While there is movement in the process of development of one's life, there is also a time for inertia where one has to slow down to listen and to be aware of what his soul is whispering in his heart. Knowledge is limited because each person only knows and understands what he had personally experienced and there is an infinite knowledge in the universe that one person cannot experience even if he will spend his whole life trying to learn all the knowledge in this vast universe that may have affect his life situations and conditions as he progresses in his development. Hence to use and exhaust all of one's knowledge is not adequate to solve a personal problem or to achieve one's goal in order to succeed, it is important for a person to consult his soul, the all-knowing soul who knows where you had been, where you are right now and where you are leading in this journey called life. Whether we do something or nothing, whether we plan or not and whether we create goals or not, life continues to move on; whether to fulfillment or miserable failures depend so much on how we manage our personal life and on our awareness of the direction in the movement and mobility of our lives. This kind of awareness needs some power beyond comprehension of a fallible mind; this is the power of guidance that is supposedly inherent in every human if we just learned how to listen to it. That's why the Bible says "There is a way that seems right unto a man but the end thereof is destruction" this only means that we tend to create and do things that we think will fill the vacuums in our lives only to find out in the end that we are still unhappy in this life; this is because we fail to consult the all-knowing soul within us; we ignore or are completely unaware of its role and power to guide us in the right paths of our journey leading to the perfect destiny of our lives in the individual level. Therefore, the most important and the wisest thing to do for a person is to learn to listen to the voice within him and make it his expertise before he would start learning the knowledge that is available in his environment.

12

MASTER OF YOUR OWN LIFE

The adage "Life is what you make it" has very important message to ponder. I would like to add too "I am the Master of my own fate" and "...We are the creators of our own luck." Many times, I heard people say "I am just not as lucky as you are Jean." Some friends would tell me that they too had done what I had been doing in my life but they just did not get so lucky as far as love in marriage, family and children, position in the job and education are concerned. A friend of mine said that she saw me as being lucky ever since we first met, she said that I was always lucky in everything that I did because according to her I am stubborn, daring, and brave. See what I mean with "we are the creators of our own luck?", her description of me as "stubborn, daring and brave" are inner qualities and power that invite luck and manifest it in our lives. I don't believe in sheer luck. If there is any luck at all, you should have invited that into your life without you even knowing it. It's your mental attitude, the energy in your mind that had accidentally invited the so-called luck to drop by in your life but notice that many of those who stumbled on sheer luck through gambling lost the money sooner than he had gotten it through "good luck" it did not stay long because the so-called luck just dropped by but once it realizes that you don't deserve it, it will quickly jump out the window of your soul and life. It reminds me of a Filipino taxi driver who won forty million pesos...such big amount of money for a person who never had such big money in his whole life. He thought that such amount is infinite and life-changing that no matter how he spends it will not run out. Within that year he bought a condominium unit worth fifteen million pesos in the heart of Manila, he also bought 20 units of taxi cabs thinking that he will have a stable income in the future from renting out those taxi cabs. There is nothing wrong in acquiring and possessing these things, what made it wrong was he started to live a life that would throw away all that he got. He let his friends drive his taxicabs and did not ask for the rent because his objective was to help those poor taxi drivers. Then his relatives who visited him increased in number; each had major financial needs such as wedding expenses for one, another was going to study college and asked him to finance him, some would like to build a house because they are homeless, another more asked for capital in a small business that he contemplated to start and more; more and more relatives, friends and even those he never met before became his relatives and friends for his "good luck" money. He was so overjoyed with his money that he felt so powerful by giving it away and spending it without limits. He started going out for fun and pleasure every night to the point that his wife and family were disappointed because he was giving away money to excessive drinking with "friends" and prostituting, he rarely come home to his wife and family, he was just overwhelmed by his new fortunate life. As a result, all his money was gone in the same year. The taxicabs needed repair and he had no more money to spend for that so he sold his condominium and all his taxicabs eventually. In the end he lost everything including his marriage and family, his "friends" and "relatives" and he went back to his old job as a taxi driver; then he said to himself "I am just born as a taxi driver, cannot be otherwise." Being the Master of your own life means that you are for yourself foremost and no matter what. If you won't stand by yourself, who will? And if you are for yourself, love yourself above all. Loving your self means knowing what your self needs before knowing the needs of others. You will be disappointed in life if you will give away everything you have, hoping that one day they will give you back what good you had given them. It does not work that way. Do some introspection and survey the contents of your heart and mind at all times.

13

MAINTAINING SELF-VALUE

Every human born in this life is a winner in his own right. Think of the millions of zygotes upon conception that race toward the fertilized egg of the mother that started life, you are one of these millions, you are the only one who made it to the egg where life started. You are the strongest, the fastest and the healthiest to win the victory medal called life, and nothing aborted you, not your mother because she had chosen to let you grow within her and you are nourished by the natural process of growth till you come out to this world as a living human. The process of growth continues, it may not be that easy at all times but you are strong enough to maintain life; you are precious and acknowledging this facts you should value yourself and your life in all areas praising the Creator for the wonder He has done, the wonder that is you. Nothing and no one can pull you down if you won't allow it. You are now the Master of your own life, yourself particularly. You have all the choices; you can decide what kind of life you should live. What kind of relationship you are going to compromise yourself with? Everything starts within you, acknowledge the beauty that is you. Appreciate the life that is you. You are not a victim of circumstances if your mind refuses to accept it. Some, if not many people would wallow in the thoughts that they are victims of circumstances such that they would feel that people around them are not good to them, that they are being neglected by their parents, that they are not the favorites of their teachers in school, that their husbands cheated on them. For those who feel that their husbands cheated on them, stop feeling sorry for yourself, you are not the one cheating, don't let the situation hurt you; you may get hurt alright, being betrayed by a person you care so much is a difficult and painful inner struggle but wake up to the fact that it can only hurt you and your life if you will allow it. You are in control of your thoughts and feelings, perhaps there is a lesson to be learned in a situation like this so instead of feeling sorry for yourself and your life, use the situation as a lesson and an opportunity to better yourself and your life. Long time ago when my first husband was still alive and we were together, I discovered one day that he was flirting with my 16-year-old housemaid, the maid admitted and told me all the details of the situation. I was terribly hurt as a result. I was feeling sorry for myself that I was not young anymore so that my husband was looking for someone younger and more exciting for him to have sex with. That was a terrible feeling and a self-defeating thought process. But one day I woke up to uphold what I really was, I stopped hurting myself, my feelings particularly and I got myself busy. I took the scholarship exam in a university which I passed with flying colors; this boost my self-esteem, it reminded me of where I was good at so I enrolled and graduated a degree eventually. Perhaps we had invited hurting circumstances in our life by forgetting our self-value. If you won't allow people to run you down, you will discover that you have something special within you that is yet to be discovered and developed for your own good. So instead of allowing bad circumstances in any area of your life constantly give you pain, discover that something good within you and focus on it once you find it. What makes you happy? Discover it instead of entertaining lingering hurt feelings that won't do you any good. Tell yourself, you are beautiful, you are smart, you are talented; that life supports itself and problems resolve themselves, just pay attention to the good things within you even if you cannot see it or you don't believe it; bluff yourself if necessary. One day you will wake up to the truth that you are actually beautiful, smart, and talented enough to make your life beautiful and meaningful. Do the affirmation, stand by yourself, appreciate your self, if you won't who will? You are your only companion in this life 24 hours a day all through the years, people come and go in your life, whether they are the ones who love and care for you or the ones that hurt you. You are the only one who stays with you and knows you inside out so take care of yourself, love yourself like you are the most valuable thing in this life because you are.

14

THREE RELIABLE INNER STRENGTHS TO SUMMON AT LIFE'S LOWEST TIMES

Life is wonderful when everything works well and you are at its peak of success. But then life's journey is full of ups and downs and twists and turns. When we are at the right path of our journey then we travel safely and swiftly; but many a times we get lost and that would start the danger that may lead us to the dead end. Wonder why many commit suicides? Imagine this situation; you are lost in a wild jungle where ferocious beasts inhabit and you cannot find your way out when suddenly right at your back is a ferocious lion ready to attack you, the natural instinct is to gather all your energy then run as fast as you can away from the chasing lion, you try to run side-ward to the left but a pack of hungry wolves see you and are preparing to attack you, you try another way turning to the right but another angry and hungry tiger is running towards you, you lift your head up hoping for a rescue but instead there's the hovering vulture waiting for your dead body so you run fast forward because you see a cliff, you had thought of just jumping down to save dear life but then a group of hungry huge crocodiles are opening their mouth expecting for your fall. That's the dead end or that's your life's ending; dead. This story is an allegory of what I had experienced some time in the past, that was exactly how I felt in my situation that I labeled my "dark ages". Why? Here are the reasons; I was completely broke and was jobless too, my husband just died leaving us nothing but hundreds of thousands of debts, and my daughter was in college, we don't even have money and source of income to support our survival needs, and we were to be evicted from our home because it's been 3 months that we were unable to pay the rent plus our electricity had been cut, we were literally living in the dark. Three hungry babies, family is broke and nobody is earning. How to survive? Good question, I did some introspection and meditation until I discovered the answers to our dilemma. First, I believe in the principle "this too will pass" that it was just one wrong turn in life's journey, a mistake and since it's a mistake it can be corrected and we can learn some valuable lessons from it. There was no easy way to get out from that situation. It was high time for me to look inside I just had to stop running and trying to evade and escape, the normal behavior in this situation would have been to go around begging for help from everyone, from friends and relatives. But then my values system won't allow me to be living the life of a mendicant, I knew there is a fountain of strength within me enough to defeat any attacks of life from any direction. The key word is Remember. Remember who you are. Remember Love. And Remember Faith. Remember who you are; in this principle I list down and write in narrative form every major positive past event of my life where I felt like I was a superstar; I remember my achievements in school where I graduated elementary as valedictorian, my being the eldest child and pampered by my parents and whole family, my happy childhood, my friends and colleagues who believed in me and my promotions and commendations at work. I kept myself busy "metaphorming" or simulating, drawing, sketching, coloring and writing down beautiful memories of my hey days, writing affirmations. I remember in details, repeating and hearing in my mind the appreciations and admiration of the people around me when they believed in me, then I thanked my God for creating me the way I am. There are always good things about us and good memories to remember. Remember love; I remember being loved by my parents and family; remember how I love them; I remember everything I value and love such as pets, work, hobbies, small possessions, God, nature and any beautiful things that attract me. Remember faith; I remember that faith is a magic word; I close my eyes and meditate seeing in my mind's eyes the beauty of life, my beautiful grandchildren wearing beautiful clothes, eating nutritious food and are very healthy. I see in my mind's eyes the transformation of my life and my family's life when the situation will change. I kept telling myself "these too will pass", "Problems resolve themselves" and "Life supports itself". The situation may not have changed abruptly but it's this process of "remembering" that kept us through during the difficult times of our lives as a family. I remember one day, when the twins were two years old, their mother went out to clean houses for the cash to buy food for the children for that day, the twins told me that they were hungry, so I asked them what they would want to eat. Moj, my little granddaughter and the girl in the boy-girl twins said that she would like to eat spaghetti; Pokoy, the grandson in the twins said that he would like to eat fried chicken. I told them to help me find a picture of those food they wanted to it from the magazines I had shown them. When they had indicated what they wanted I cut them out and pasted them on a hardboard, I decorated it then made it into a poster as I posted it on the wall of my bedroom. I told them to make a sound together like they were chanting. I had read somewhere in one of my books the chant that says "Om mani padme aum", I let them memorize that and that was what we three were chanting as we face the poster of the food on the wall. It did not take very long when I heard a call from outside, the janitor in the Pro-Gloria Headquarter; this was a political headquarter during election campaign season, the office was just across our apartment; the janitor was outside the door, he was carrying many small Styrofoam boxes of food, he said that the man in-charge of the office sent him to deliver the food because McDonald gave him too much food he cannot eat them all and also he thought the children might like them; McDonald being the sponsor of the party supplied them food every day, there were a dozen boxes of spaghetti and fried chicken plus rice in those boxes. We were excited and much more, it was just the beginning, every day there excess of food supply in that office so they us food every day and aside from that I was hired to work in that office as in-charge of the distribution of all the election paraphernalia. Being head of the office, I was to hire temporary employees to distribute the paraphernalia to the public so I hired my daughter-in-law and my daughter. We all had jobs this time and the children never get hungry again. I know how faith works and I know in my heart completely that problems resolve themselves and both good and difficult times pass, nothing is permanent.

15

A MEDITATION PRACTICE

What is meditation and why do we need it? Meditation is paying attention to your inner and Higher Self. It is prayer in a meditative form. It is your way to self-awareness, to know what goes within you. It is common knowledge that human beings are not just body, we got souls and spirit. If we take care of our physical health that we nourish our body with healthy food it is also equally important to nourish our soul and spirit; knowing our desires, our inner strength and weaknesses is prerequisite to a healthy living, abundant life in all areas, peace, and complete happiness.

Meditation is emptying the mind, body and heart from any concerns in your material world. This is the time to invoke your Higher Self to take charge of your life especially when you had done all the logical thinking and nothing happens.

Following is the basic of all my meditation practices;

I go to a quiet place alone; I sit in a lotus position or lie down in silence; I breath rhythmically as I slowly close my eyes; I am now relaxing my body and my mind; I am now aware of my slowing pulse beats Unwinding and relaxing more and more in each rhythmic breath I am now one with myself; It's only me, my life and nothing else.

My body is now feeling lighter and lighter; A Light appears inside my forehead between my brows; It is moving fast, changing forms from tiny dots to spirals of smoke To triangles, shadows, brightness and various colors traversing and mixing to create forms; Then some specific forms appear like clear photographs of places, people, events and objects; I just watch them, I am detached, no feelings, no interpretations, just watch as I continue to relax with my slow breath.

Gradually and tenderly, I focus my mind to things that I want to see and do; Observing my feelings; some feelings of delight and desires; Then the visions appear just as I want them to be; Feelings of love, beauty, admiration, and joy gradually enfold me; I am now deep within my soul; To the core and nucleus of my existence; Meeting my Higher Self and the Divine within me; Awaiting the Divine Guidance and Message; I am now connected to the Source of all Life; I am one with the Universe; Divine Light is Guiding me now; I am now attuned to the Divine Plan of my life; Divine Love is opening the way for me; He is showing me the way now; He walks before me and leads me on; He is now creating miracles in my mind, in my body, and in all my affairs.

Now I am enjoying the beauty of nature, including me; I now see and feel the beauty of life within me; My life is precious along with the rest of all creations; I am one with the Light; I feel God's overflowing love for me; All the love I need is already within my own heart; I now share it to everyone. Everything that I need to sustain my precious life and to make my life full of bliss that I can channel to everyone concerned; Is already within me and would manifest in my material plane in perfect timing.

I now open my eyes and I'm wide awake; To the material plane of my existence; I feel so refreshed from that journey within me; The Higher part of me where I draw my strength for my everyday life; I am strong knowing that deep within me is the source of what I manifest in the material world; I have the balance and equilibrium of my consciousness as I live my life along with all creatures in this universe. I know that God's Will works powerfully in my life. I now accept and receive my blessings and share them to all; For the highest good of all concerned. So be it. So it is.

16

Greater Than You Can Imagine

Following are two short poems to remind ourselves that envy and jealousy has no place in our mind, in our heart and in our lives consecutively if we keep on dreaming and on living our dreams. These poems are self-reminders too that there is something for each of us in this universe and that each of us vary in perfect timing depending on individual differences in all our personality make-up. We are all here for good reasons; let's just live our lives and enjoy what the universe has granted us in our every here and now.

Greater than You can Imagine

Life is full of intervals and paradoxes;
Now you are on top, tomorrow where could you be?
It's maybe a dark night for me;
But for sure I live to welcome the new day.
You showed me your huge bank balance; your valuable possessions and top achievements;

Your regal mansion, jewelry, yacht, helicopters, jaguars and Cadillac, medals and trophies;

All these to spite me because you see my deprivation as mediocrity.

If I am short of intuition, insight and foresight I would have knelt down before you in awe, adoration or perhaps envy and jealousy with such self-pity.

But I am sorry to disappoint you because I know something that is greater than you can imagine.

It is powerful, it lives, lives within me and we have such intimacy which assures me of my own greatness, the greatness that is higher and loftier than what you can show me.

I have dreams and desires awaiting manifestations in perfect timing.

This universe has riches great enough for everyone to partake and enjoy.

I have just discovered self-awareness and the Source of wealth that come to me in manifold.

I have just experienced the Oneness with the Mind that is Greater than you can Imagine.

Awake My Beloved

Awake my Beloved!
It's been so long in the slumber-land;
Stretch your strong muscles now;
Stand tall and run the race before you!
The goal is just a few steps away;
Move on and reach your Mega Star;
Deep within me you've been dormant; the loudest gongs

had been sounded; I am eager as before to watch again your achievements;

Show off your magnificence!
Reign victorious for the rest of your days.
Remember your greatness!
Awake now for Life's sake!

17

ORDER OF LIFE

Life evolves going through various stages of development. Human beings differ in development and success depending on culture and nature of each individual. You can see for example in the development of babies, some babies start walking at 6 months, 8 months 10 months or one year. Not all babies could start walking at the same age, even in speaking, some could speak earlier and others in a very later stage of development. There is a certain order and stage of development that we follow in the individual differences of development. Nature hates uniformity, nature is all beauty and it advocates variation and harmony in its midst. There is variation and harmony in the order of life as determined by nature hence one cannot envy the success of another in certain areas of life even when he fails in the same area because we all differ in everything especially in our perception of things around us and on certain inner developments.

Following is a poem that shows people's shortsightedness in this natural order of life.

Order of Life

You keep running here and there;

You are not even chasing rainbows;

You run without a direction, you just spin 'round and 'round;

You fear your shadow; It follows you wherever you are;

And so, you run as fast as you can and as far can be;

You stumbled, collapsed then awaken only to continue running around' and 'round once more.

You run away again from your own shadow; wondering why it sticks with you, the one that you fear most.

You run to the broad light of day but you see nothing;

Except the monstrous shadow that the light creates;

You take shield in darkness for the shadow to disappear;

But the cold and chill paralyze your marrows;

Even your scream won't let out from your frozen throat;

Choked by the endless darkness in the night of your life.

The cares of life overwhelm you;

Anxiety grips your core;

Your mind is numbed and cloudy;

So, you locked yourself into the darkest corner of your existence;

As you turn away from your truth; then you close your eyes in order to forget;

Oh, feeble mind, when will you come to terms with yourself?

Don't you ever realize that the shadow has no essence and is powerless to destroy you?

Why are you hiding in that cloak and facade of retardation?

Shadows are there to announce the exact time of day;
And to urge you to move on to a sure destination.

Stop making them a monster; Thus, keeping you away
from your unfolding truth;

Welcome the world of colors, shapes, clarity and natural
beauty.

Stop running to and fro;
Think and be reasonable;
What are your desires?
Know yourself and start from there;
Accept your truth and let it unfold in its own phase;
Create the life you contemplate and focus on it;
Think. Think. Think.

Think on how you can achieve your dreams. Look
around and look good!

Look for the materials and tools to build your dream;
This world is in abundance to meet your every need.

Just look and see;
Look up to your star;
Look up to the sun of your existence;
It gives you the brightest light that even the shadow
cannot persist.

The energy from the sun makes everything possible for
you; feel it, know it, embrace it;

The darkness is made for you to rest;
Sleep peacefully in the night; And work joyfully during
the day;

Only then could you have a balanced life;
If you follow the order that your life should be.

18

JUST A PASSERBY

"This world is not my home."

I consider myself lucky or blessed for so many reasons. I can count and enumerate my blessings, but that's beside the point. In my childhood and before I was at age fifteen "exiled" to become a Missionary; my family, consisting of Dad, Mum, sister Leah, and brother Jun, spent at least one-month summer vacation in the farm every year. Our farm was called Chile Valley, to honor Brother Raul Escobar from Chile.

He was the first Missionary of the International Missionary Society to come to the Philippines and who converted my Dad to become a Missionary himself. My Dad was one of the two pioneering Filipino missionaries under this organization. The foreigner Missionaries such as Andrade, Pizzarro, Abraham, Nicolicci, Kozel, among others, frequented our beautiful farm and I grew up mingling with them. Being the eldest child, I was center of attention to my Dad's frequent visitors and colleagues; he bragged me to them, not that I was happy about that; I was made to recite three chapters of Bible verses to the missionaries, and a lot more show offs about me as presented by my Dad to his comrades. It is ironic that my Dad had properties but in our family worship hour done twice a day, every 5:00 to 6:00 a.m. and p.m., my Dad would lead us in singing "This world is not my home I am just passing by..." and also "I am a stranger here within a foreign land, my home is far away upon the golden strand; Ambassador to be in realms beyond the sea, I'm here on business for my King."

While I was far from home being in the IMS (International Missionary Society), Manila as a Colporteur my Dad also started his "nomadic" life, tagging along my siblings and Mum as they were assigned to several places around the country as a missionary family. One of my Dad's favorite verses from the Bible which he often recited to us every worship time is "Those who cannot leave his land, house, family, in my name are not worthy of me...", I learned to hate this verse. Because of this fanatic conversion of my Dad, he distributed his land to 30 poor families and left only a 6-hectare parcel of farm which he entrusted to his brother Tirso, who, himself had a ten-hectare farm of his own. He also sold our two houses in the city then joined the missionary work as a volunteer. When I came home from the missionary work, I was met by a very different home life situation. Gone were the comforts of home and found my family living in my uncle's house.

"This too will pass."

That background of my life had long passed and I am in my "here and now". The shoes I wore when I was six years old, even if it's still good and usable, I cannot wear them now that I am 62. We change along with the passing of time, not just physically but also intellectually, otherwise we will be intellectual "bonsais".

We change not only physically but also intellectually and, in our values system, viewpoints and core beliefs. What I used to believe when I was 15 years old and was with my family is not what I believe now. We can change our belief system otherwise we will just be a beautiful but callous and empty-headed manikin.

Everything that we had been through passed away as we continue to live and evolve until our time will come to pass away too. We all had been through a lot of situations in life, some situations call for celebrations and are full of excitement, other situations are sadness and loss but they all pass away. Some experiences make us honorable and dignified; others are embarrassing and a disgrace. These are experiences in life that all pass by. Some friends and love ones leave this life ahead of us. They had been into lots of happiness and joy in this life. They had possessed material good and had achieved success in life in their own rights. They also had experienced a lot of problems that are sometimes, if not often, seem unbearable; but everything passes by including each of them.

Living in my "here and now."

This phrase from the poem, "The Miller of the Dee" and I quote, "...I envy nobody and nobody envies me..." is worth pondering. If we live in the "here and now" life could be meaningful and worth-living. What are the things to do in the "here and now" that can make life meaningful? Living in the "here and now" means appreciating our value as a person in a moment by moment basis. All things come and go, all experiences pass by, people come and people go nobody stays with us permanently even our own children.

Then what is left with us? with you? My good friend and colleague, Ma'am Semeramis Bamba, died of lung cancer years back, she was just 50. She is 5 years younger than me. She was a brilliant English Professor. She had everything, 2 beautiful grandchildren, three beautiful and educated daughters, a prestigious position in school...the list could go on. She never smoked and was a perfectionist in all her ways...and she was near to perfection in her looks and beauty...such a waste for a brilliant and beautiful human. Two days before she died, Ma'am Veron and I visited her in the hospital and her last words to us, to me specifically...

"...Ma'am Jenny, you are one of my source of inspiration when something confuses me...but you smoke and never have cancer whereas I am careful in my food and I never smoke but look at me; you are carefree, you get angry when you want, you laugh when you feel good, you have the presence of mind and an assertiveness that anyone can wonder, you love and you are loved...you never suppress your emotions and that makes you significant from the rest of us...I wish I could turn back the time so I can live in my here and now full of freedom rather than full of restrictions and plans that never work."

I never realized how I scored with my colleagues but from the mouth of a dying dear friend. I consider life as just a dream. My every here and now is a dream; Today is the manifestation of what I dreamed yesterday; I don't know exactly what tomorrow is; But I know that the beautiful dream I dream today is the beautiful tomorrow that would come my way. So, my "here and now is a beautiful dream." That kind of dream that would be my tomorrow's "here and now." Like everybody else I am just a passerby in this life...the life that is just a dream; like a dream that fades like bubbles, is what life and everything in it, is all about.

19

Choose to Remember

Every person alive had been through a lot of ups and downs and twists and turns in life, no one is exempted. No matter how careful a person is there is always a time in his life that he feels sad and empty. Those we see as being happy and in great abundance and looking loved and cared for in a given time must have also experienced some low points in life in the past. Whether real or perceived or imaginary, these low points are real for the person in question. No one is exempted because life is movement and development even if we want to believe that there is stability if we just follow the rules. The rule is "CHANGE" and "MOVEMENT" but then we don't have to panic because we are also equipped with antidotes to counter and to straighten every turn that happens in our lives. All we need to do is to summon these tools to your rescue and protection in order to survive and to continue moving on. The fact is everything passes; sadness, happiness, griefs, even abundance. When you are at the top you can expect to fall by a single wrong step but that's not the end unless you die by that fall. That is the reason why we have to celebrate life because life means continuous movement towards your destiny while you still have it.

During one of those low times of my life I had this experience and the poem was made to remind me that it was not the end of the world for me, I am still alive and I have gone a long way since then.

Language of My Soul at The Time

My New Zealander husband Adrian Shiels, died in 2003 but he had been bedridden for two years till the end. I wrote the following narrative to myself on January 4, 2001 when I had to quit my job to take care of him full time. It was among the lowest point of my life and I felt so isolated considering the many years I spent in the academe as a professor, in my Masters studies and other social activities. I just share it here in a narrative poetic form to remind everyone that life have twists beyond human control regardless of the best efforts we offer for its enjoyment and success. This poem is also a reminder that we have to embrace life including the pain and the sorrows that may pass our way. Each person must be the number one fan and lover of himself, otherwise, who else will? I entitled this narrative poem "Choose to Remember," here it goes;

Choose to Remember

Why are you so sad my dearest?
You look so awful;
You don't take a bath;
You don't comb your hair;
You don't wash your face;
Your dirty and skinny face sags;

You don't even change your clothes for many days;

Look in the mirror; your sunken eyes are fixed to nowhere; your brows meet; your forehead wrinkles, you look a century older;

Your lips are pouting and dry; have you anything for your stomach yet?

Is this how you want yourself to look?

Why do you brood and sulk?

Sitting down in the dark corner of this cold room with bowed head and drooping shoulders;

Bent long knees reaching above your head;

How long have you been in this condition? Days? Months? Years?

You don't go out any more like you used to do; you don't talk to people who are more in need for your words of comfort;

You are so dysfunctional even for your personal well-being.

What is the big deal?

Is it because you believe that nobody cares for you?

Is it because you are convinced that nobody remembers you?

Is it a feeling of rejection?

Is it deprivation of material possessions?

Or is it a belief that you are a failure or a loser in life?

Is it a feeling that you are at a dead-end in life's journey?

What exactly is it that brought you to this miserable state?

That you just have to drift to nothingness making your life worthless in the process?

Do you feel that all your dreams and wishes had turned to ashes?

Now, my Beloved, take a long deep breath;

Listen to my counsel once and for all.

You still have the mind, it's your tool to remember what you really are, a tool to lift you up from misery; use it if it's just for now.

Remember how you used to be; how you always are yesterday, today and through eternity;

Recall what you used to teach me on life's reality.

Do you remember who you are?

Remember your natural state of being;

"I am a survivor" remember saying this?

Remember you are an asset, a treasure and a joy to those around you?

Remember your inheritance?

Remember your true love? Your feelings of love?

Remember who loves you with such unconditional love?

Remember He delights in serving you?

Remember He provides everything for you "according to His riches in glory"?

Start looking at the brighter side of life.

Notice that the dark side is there to illumine the light;

Just choose to remember that the sun rises after the darkest dawn.

Remember that the most powerful weapon against darkness is to shine.

Fear not the shadows, don't let them bother you, never allow them to pull you down, use them as your footstool instead to catapult you to the brightest star above.

Arise now My Beloved!

Clean up and purge yourself.

Choose gladness and a merry heart; whistle a tune or two if you must.

Choose wisdom and discernment.

Re-enlist and summon your bright experiences of joy and success.

Choose love and compassion;

Choose forgiveness and peace;

Choose hope and faith;

Choose to believe;

Choose dignity, health, beauty and prosperity;

Choose goodness and kindness;

Focus your mind to the Light within you;

Only then will the shadows disappear;

So choose to remember.

Remember now?

Sometimes, only us (you, I) can lift us up from life's miseries. Everything we need is already within us, if we just choose to remember...remember that even the darkest cloud has its silver lining.

20

MY INVISIBLE LITTLE WORLD

In the past, before para normal Science had announced to the world through self-help books that fantasy and imagination are good tools to keep life going...people are ashamed to even create imaginary reality that exist only in their minds. Where do all these paintings of great artists come from, and all the fantastic fairy tales? Didn't they come from richly imaginative minds of the artists and writers? Children and teen-age people have very rich imaginations and in the past many people would think that to imagine is useless and non-productive...and would brush it off as "it's just an imagination" which means that it cannot come true. I read a book about imagery that tells of many relevance of imagination as having helped a person heal his illness, winning an athletic game among others. To imagine and fantazise is to help ourselves escape from the harsh reality of the present situation that castigate us in certain low times of our lives. When nothing else helps, use your imagination...it would do wonders in your life...trust me in this.

A narrative poem.

I wrote this narrative poem on June 2, 2002 when I

was jobless because I was care-giving full time to my then bedridden husband, Adrian Shiels. He died ten months later. I share this experience as an example of a good imagination that could help us through the darkness of our lives that may befall us. In times when there is nothing you can do anymore to change your difficult situation, go deep down within you and create a beautiful world of your own. It's free to dream and God knows what comes next, the idea is to enjoy life even if it is only in your imagination.

My Invisible Little World

Beyond anyone else's understanding and imagination;
Lies my invisible little world.
No one can reach it; It's farther than the least visible star on a clear starry night;
It lies in the depths beyond the deepest ocean floor; It's nowhere even in the earth's core.
No one knows of its existence;
Nobody has even thought about it; If there was one to sense of its existence then he must be a psychic;
Yet it does exist in anyone alive.
Doesn't everybody's beliefs base on his experience?
Those that can be seen, heard, and the rest of the senses?
My invisible world is me, my mind, my emotions, and the complete me.
My invisible world is a perfectly beautiful and harmonious kingdom;
I am the crowned and honorable queen;
My king's throne and my own are set side by side;
My adorable king adores me as much;

We are soul-mates that hail from time immemorial;

He delights in me, he loves me, he serves me and pampers me;

My king is my life and so am I to him;

Nothing can come between us;

Death is powerless; for my king and I are inseparable.

There is love beyond compare in my invisible little world.

My invisible little world is an untouched paradise of beauty and abundance; My court servants are angels and cherubim and sage; They sing to the voice of rain and thunder a-blending; They dance with the gracefulness of the cool breeze;

They play the harp with the soothing and harmonic melodies of the rushing creek; Such pleasure beyond compare in my invisible little world.

My mentors and sources of knowledge and wisdom are the wiz of the ancient worlds beyond the sky;

They tell of a land where fire and water mix;

They tell of a love, a hope, and a courage, that create the universe;

They tell of alpha and omega, of unending stories of subjects beyond human discernment;

Such joy beyond compare in my invisible little world.

In my invisible little world, everybody loves everybody;

Everybody makes everybody happy;

Everybody appreciates everybody's uniqueness;

Everybody is vibrantly healthy and radiantly beautiful;

Everybody is a genius and talented;

Criticism is an alien in my invisible world;

Comparison and condemnation are outsiders;

Everybody and everything are just perfectly beautiful and harmonious.

My invisible little world is not a Utopia; It's a fact;

Of course, you can laugh;

How can a born-blind person understand red when all his life everything is black?

He can laugh to his heart's satisfaction, despite his predicament, if someone insists to him the existence of any color;

He cannot even understand black even if that is his only world because color is just beyond his nature and he's got no point of comparison.

So is everybody who heard my story of my invisible little world. Did you say that I am living in fantasy?

That I am deluded or idealistic?

Whatever you call it, the fact remains that the outside world, is now filled with comfort and convenience, Because of the people who were once called Crazy, lunatic, deluded; When they were just bringing out the existence of their invisible little world.

Try to turn the pages of history;

Read the life of the ineducable idiot Thomas Edison;

The two brothers who died and whose death contributed to make the world smaller by reaching far destinations by flying.

My invisible little world is a universe. Discover that within you my friend. For God's sake!

21

I Am a Traveler

This poem which I wrote years back in Hubpages is symbolic of a person's deep longings and on his search for happiness in this life; it is also symbolic to the nature of life which is MOVEMENT. Life is movement, a journey and a destiny; this is what this poem is all about.

Destiny?

From my native land I fled, to the Land of Promise beyond;

It will take me a lifetime, conditions, emotions, and lots of decision-making before I could ever reach my destiny;

The Destiny that is drawing me closer but never arriving there.

Why must I leave?

Don't I have love ones who gladly accommodate and cheer me?

I can choose to stay and try to feel good about it;

My native land has its own culture;

People here get along well;

There is plenty of food, drinks, jobs, abundance of love and camaraderie;

I can live forever here and be merry for the rest of my life;

Everything I need is already here;

My native land is a wonderful place to raise a family;

A few get rich and almost everyone seems happy and contented;

The Leaders who govern the masses are idolized and are the ideals of the citizenry;

They are the law, the status quo and the models of society;

Why can't I just stay and comply?

Who knows what comes out here for me?

But I am a traveler; my parents were too;

They just happened to make this place one of their stopovers during my birth;

And they stayed too long, long enough for both of them to die here and for me to forget of my true origin;

They got very busy establishing rapport with the natives here;

The inhabitants here benefited from their creativity;

They had gathered treasures for themselves from the rich resources in this God-given blessed land;

The people loved them so much;

My parents had built their mansion here and before they died, they were able to distribute their properties and share their blessings to the peasants.

But I am a traveler, it's in my blood;

Now that I am on my own, I must continue the journey that had been long interrupted;

I have to survey the world and discover new things in different lands and people;

That is my mission as a traveler;

I will achieve the objective of the mission that my parents had chosen to forget;

My accomplishments, achievements and experiences with people, both natives and travelers,

and with nature along the way;

Make my life worth-living.

If I'd prefer to stay, it would only be an empty body;

Because my heart, my mind, and my soul take me to distant lands;

To be with other travelers like me;

Who always long to be home;

To be home in the Promised Land;

To be with the King of kings of my Destiny;

He is the King of the Promised Land, the King of the Ultimate Destiny

Where everyone alive both people and everything in this vast universe are destined;

I have to go ahead;

And perform my mission;

For I was born to achieve and to lighten the hearts of other travelers

Who continue searching for the meaning of life, the now and the beyond?

My travels may be full of adventures, pleasant or unpleasant;

But my reward will be the crown from the King

Who is all-knowing and Omnipotent;

This is my mission; I am a traveler.

22

POWERFUL FEELINGS

Feelings

Who can truly understand the feelings within me?

Can anyone see that my <u>feelings</u> are life itself that can control me?

My feelings are sensitive and responsive to my thoughts, perceptions and interpretations of things around me;

My feelings react to situations, people, places, events, and conditions that surround me;

They react to temperatures, weather and anything that could be felt or sensed.

My feelings are so delicate and tender yet also vehement and explosive;

They are the index of my very soul;

And must be guided and guarded for they are so powerful.

How I live my life and my lifestyle is the product of the moment feelings and the feelings that I accumulate within me;

My total personality depends so much on my emotional state in a given moment;

My moment by moment feelings can lead to achievements or failures as the case maybe;

To <u>creativity</u> and productivity or to failures and destruction depending on the feelings I constantly keep within me and express outwardly;

My feelings compel me to behave and act accordingly in a given time and place with certain conditions and people;

My beautiful and positive feelings in a given time and space, reflect to everyone around me;

Everybody would feel wonderful and life will be blessed;

But if ugly and negative feelings prevail in me for long, life for everyone, including my own and my love ones would be miserable;

Ow, it is therefore important that my feelings must be under God's guidance and control.

Suppressing my feelings makes my life bitter and worst later;

It's like hiding rotten vegetables and dead animals in a vacuumed closet;

Where worms and maggots produce poisoned gasses and deadly odors;

To gradually consume the soul.

Even beautiful feelings such as love and compassion; if denied due expression Would be like hiding burning coals under a pile of fresh leaves and grasses inside a box of rubbish;

Sooner the smoke comes out followed by explosive heat Which eventually turn into fire and destruction of lives around it.

When I feel very tired and confused that make me dysfunctional

Then I know for sure that deep within me are feelings that are ignored.

Headaches, stomachaches, body aches, fatal diseases such as tumors and cancers can be results of anger, resentments, frustrations, rejections and anguish of the soul.

Worries and anxieties if not checked and resolved lead to wasted lives and failures;

Hurting feelings such as guilt, <u>betrayals</u>, hatred, jealousy, envy, fear, inadequacy, being misunderstood and maltreated must be faced squarely and be brought out to its proper place and perspective;

The mind is equipped with necessary tools to combat these dark and destructive feelings;

Let the mind summon all its forces to blot out and dissolve these feelings of doom.

Hurt feelings are heavy and burdensome; they wear down the soul;

But I am greater than my feelings, and even greater than my mind;

I am the Master of my soul.

I have to check my feelings every now and then before they could reproduce and create a clan within me;

I have to be aware of their presence and their effects in me and on my life as a whole;

So many lives had been destroyed by uncontrolled and unguarded feelings;

Broken homes and crimes to mention a few;

I have to scrutinize their nature until there is nothing of their sorts are left in me;

Only then could I purge myself and begin to shine.

And when the Light within me shines brightly;

The Light that emanates from the Divine Source;

All the shadows and darkness caused by hurting feelings will be gone;

I am myself once more;

I just have to acknowledge my feelings as part of me;

Select the good feelings and let it stay;

Recognize those feelings that could hurt and banish them away.

Peace, joy, hope, faith, forgiveness, and <u>love</u> are the only feelings that I keep.

23

MY LIFE IS SHAPED
BY MY CHOICES

Life is what we make it. This article is all about the decisions we make in every turn of the way as we journey on in this life. We make choices in any given situation of our life. Life has many choices and in making those choices you need to be aware of what you really want and what you deserve in this life. Self-awareness is very important otherwise if you live your life depending on someone else' decision you won't be happy. Lots of people will come to a point where they say "I have no choices" this is a dead-end statement; there are always many choices in life in all areas. We often make wrong decisions and make mistakes. Some mistakes are small and can easily be straightened but some are big enough to change the direction of our lives toward more and more mistakes that make us feel like failures and useless in this life. That is why self-awareness is very important, it guides us to the right direction so that we can acknowledge any time that we are already sidetracking hence we can immediately correct our own mistakes before everything turns into out of control situation. Every mistake we do have consequences that we suffer. The bigger the mistake the bigger too is the punishment and these punishments cost us time and misery if we are lucky to be still alive. To make mistakes is human and we must not be afraid to make one, the good news is we can always choose to forgive ourselves then correct the mistake as soon as you recognize it then continue moving on in the right direction.

Self-Awareness

"My decisions are statements of my identity; Every decision I make embodies my self-concept and my view of the world; Choices are not mere isolated events on the periphery of my life, rather choices are my life. Good decisions are my true thoughts and feelings; my beliefs and emotions that draw vital wisdom inherent in me. I am conscious of my motivations. I am aware of the beliefs that propel me toward or away from what I truly desire or my goals and dreams; I am always Divinely-guided and my spiritual awareness leads me to the fulfilling life that I deserve."

Below are two important choices that you can do namely "chasing rainbows" and making goals"

People are busy "chasing rainbows" What are most people busy about?

Most people are busy searching on how to get or earn more money, whether in the Net or in real life situation. Everything they do is always a byproduct of their persistence to get more money. It's not bad actually, when they do it in all honesty of intention; it is valid when they do it with integrity and without molesting or destroying other people's works and lives. I advocate Divine Guidance in securing a life of abundance rather than on "chasing rainbows" method of acquiring wealth...remember that the more you chase anything the faster it evades you and flee away from you. I like these lines of a song; I added more words based on my experiences; "Are you tired of chasing pretty rainbows? Are you tired of spinning round and round? Lay down your dreams and submit it to the Greatest Intelligence that knows better than you can ever know in your lifetime."

Each of us lives our lives by following certain sets of patterns that our psyche had perceived and set for us as a result of our imaginations, choices, decision-making and actual life experiences over the years. Life is full of complexities that it is difficult to focus on a goal that we supposedly desire to achieve. In the first place, even to create a goal is complicated by itself. Even in the idea of creating a goal is already a difficult task because it needs certain degree of conviction within us, otherwise fear gets in the way; that fear of not achieving the goal is by itself a block to create a goal. Many people try to create a goal but deep within them is a feeling which says, it's just a goal, I am not one hundred percent sure that I can achieve it.

Dreams and goals

What choices do you have? What are your goals?

There are as many goals as there are many needs, wants, desires, and urges in the individual levels. Lots of people get mixed up in their goals for education and career, money and income, self-esteem or socialization and status quo, health or fitness and beauty, relationships and romance, socialization, comfort and self-actualization; the list could go on to infinity.

Goals undergo certain processes starting from; 1. why the goal was created 2. what specific goal to focus in a specific time and place 3. the advantages and disadvantages in setting such a goal 4. setting alternative courses of actions to pursue such a goal 5. the pros and cons of a chosen alternative 6. strategies of implementing the chosen course of action.

And these are just among other things that any sensible person can do. What about those who never bother to create a goal in the first place because they have such mental attitude as to just exist and follow whatever society is set for them? What will happen to the definition of man as a sentient being? Man, as a thinking being? Even "to think" or "not to think" is a matter of choice. "To think" is to set goals for one's self in any area of one's existence. "Not to think" means, "to just drift in life wherever it may lead him and to follow what everybody else thinks and do." It's easier to imitate or duplicate than to design, create and to be original in any area of one's life.

Given these two choices; chasing rainbows and creating goals, which would you prefer?

24

Manifestation Process: My Story

What would you feel if one of your most important dreams had come true? You must feel blessed and blissful or lucky; and what if all of your dreams or anything that you wish for and desire has come to material reality? You will really feel very lucky in life, for life! and would enjoy every moment that you have, whether you are alone or with many people. You would feel rich, beautiful, lovable, and lucky and would say life is wonderful. Once you learn and know that you can easily manifest everything that you desire or that you can easily make all your dreams come true, you would never stop creating dreams or goals because you know they would all come true. But it is sad to know that there are so many quotes and messages that are spread in the net which says to the effect "not all you want in life could happen to you or could be yours" "you have to accept and be contented with your bitter lot in life" and so on, and amazingly most people accept these as true and they believe in all these limiting concepts. To have expertise in manifestation and manifesting all you want is a special talent and a blessing but could you believe that you too can acquire such ability? You cannot even believe that such talent exists especially when you had been through a lot of frustrations and disappointments in life. The ability to manifest what you truly desire for your self can be developed but first you have to believe and be deeply convinced that this talent is inherent in every person alive including you. "Necessity is the mother of invention" this statement proves right to me. I noticed that whenever I had a need or when I was in difficult times in any area of my life, my mind wanders and would think on how I can get out of the situation until I discovered that something within me can do the seemingly impossible things for me at a moment to set me free.

First I discovered the fact that "problems resolve themselves" and that "life supports itself" and also that "this too will pass" meaning even the most difficult and overwhelming situations in our lives at a certain time will not stay long because we have the definite ability to banish them away. I also learned from experience that our core beliefs and principles in life are the controlling factors that govern our life situations at all times.

It was one of the lowest point of my life financially, jobless therefore broke but my faith was bigger than our situation. I took a pen and a notebook and wrote down the affirmations as follow "I, Jenny, now have a good job that I love doing by which I am well-compensated." I wrote this in first, second and third person 20 times. While I was writing my daughter was washing her clothes downstairs preparing them for her plan to look for a job that week, it was a Monday. Before going down to start washing her clothes she assured me that I didn't have to work because I was already old, I was 50 at that time, and further said that it's her turn to take responsibility of the household and to take care of me, she added further that she can afford to support me once she gets a job and that it would be easier for her to get a job because she is young and having a degree; in the Philippines there is a rampant age discrimination in finding a job. My daughter is truly God's precious gift to my life, she is always sweet, good-nature and having a kind-heart.

I was still writing my affirmation when my daughter's mobile rang so she ran up the stairs to the second floor of the apartment where she left her mobile. The Pastor of the church, Pastor Calalang called her and asked her if she was interested to teach English to Korean high school students and if she is she can start working that same day in the afternoon; the salary was to be five thousand pesos a month and she would only teach four hours a day; for a fresh graduate it was a good deal as far as my daughter is concerned. She was so excited to break the news to me as I was equally excited as well. But when I asked if five thousand pesos can already support our needs and the bills, reminding her that the rent alone was three thousand pesos, so could the remaining two thousand pesos be enough for the bills and our survival needs, she assured me that she will find a second job by tutoring other Korean students. I believed my daughter, she had a very good reputation to the Koreans, they like her and many would call her and ask her to do tutorial jobs for them, besides my daughter is very hard-working, she had started tutorial job even before she graduated a degree and her good reputation started from there.

That afternoon my daughter started working and at 5:00 o'clock her job was done and came home straight with another good news. She said that the Korean Director asked her to help him find a Filipino teacher who is experienced in teaching and has a Master's degree in teaching English (TESL)and who is also a licensed teacher, meaning who had passed the PBET (Philippine Board Examination for Teachers), immediately my daughter replied, "that's my Mom; she has a Master's degree in (TESL) and she is a licensed teacher having passed the (PBET) with 10 years' experience in teaching high school and college." To shorten the story, the next day it was not just my daughter who went to work in the same school, the bonus is, I was given ten thousand pesos monthly salary hence doubling my daughter's for teaching just two hours a day; I was teaching college.

The financial difficulty that my daughter and I were supposed to face in the immediate future didn't happen. We didn't even have to look for a job, we attracted the job because we had established a reputation and I would still attribute this incident to my affirmations.

Coincidence? Not so, lots of people in our qualifications would spend weeks, even months and lots of rejections before they can get a job. My psyche presented the opportunity that knocked on our door, this time rang the phone to present itself to us.

I would reiterate the benefits we get which I discussed in my previous article about writing affirmations into making it a habit. The psyche would learn to instantaneously respond to your needs when it arises because it had stocks of wisdom in your mind's "cabinet."

25

A Blueprint for Your Life

When I was 16 years old and working as a Colporteur missionary in IMS (International Missionary Society) I came across this statement from one of my readings "Plan your work and work your plan." This statement became my railing in everything that I was doing since then. Years later when I studied MBA, I learned more thoroughly the importance of planning when you have certain projects which you want to succeed.

Planning is the first step to success for how can you succeed in something that never even had a goal in the first place. So, in terms of your life, do you have plans, or a plan? A plan is good but to succeed is to be thorough in working out for such plan to reach its goals. A comprehensive plan should include all the details from goal-setting to strategies and implementations that should be followed through or monitored to see that you are in the right track.

Your plan should follow the blueprint that you have created for yourself and your life. A blueprint is actually the framework where you should fill in the plans when needs arise and in which your plan should be based in every detail. Here I draw a symbolical framework that I can see every day to remind me that I will only do things that are within this framework. This symbolic framework is for myself; anybody can be creative and make their own; what is important is you understand all the symbols and that they are meaningful to you.

The following are eight symbolical components of a complete framework that I made for the kind of life that I intend to create for myself within a given period of time. I had made a drawing that symbolizes these eight components of my life's framework. This drawing is shown here as an example.

1. Abundance... Abundance is symbolized here by the branch of a tree that is full of fruits and a basket. The basket represents labor or work to harvest naturally its fruit. Natural abundance is represented by the tree which is directly connected to the ground, the "mother" earth.

2. Love... Love is represented by the symbol yin and yang. This shows that love relationship can only be fulfilling and successful when there is perfect reciprocity.

3. Peace... Peace here is represented by a dove with young fresh leaves.

4. Beauty... There are seven stars with colors different from one another and they are shown like coming from far away to the present. Significant to this is the sexy body of a woman, which for me would mean my sexuality and being sensuous; these are necessary feminine characteristics when used

in a natural sense as represented by the flowers, the landscape, the sky, water. Sexuality should be naturally productive and must be in its proper perspective rather than abused to insinuate others.

5. Health... Health symbol here is the restoration to the natural flow from within and outward.

6. Success... Success is represented by a bird in paradise that had finally reach the sun, the source of energy and the peak of one's potentials.

7. Happiness... Happiness is represented by a woman who is capable of leaping over obstacles. She is backed up by the source of energy, the sun.

8. Faith... Faith is the eyes that can see beyond what the immediate environment is presenting; it's wisdom.

26

THE MAGIC OF WRITING AN IDEAL SCENE 02/20/17

Like writing affirmations writing an ideal scene has a magical effect once your psyche becomes convinced and amenable to it. An ideal scene is a picture in your mind, a scenario where you can see clearly your new life once your dream comes true. You can write and describe the details of that scene or you can collect pictures of yourself and put it in the center of a poster where all the pictures surrounding it are the ones you had dreamed off. In 2013, I wrote my ideal scene as follows, this one is concerning my husband and I living together in America. At that time I became hopeless to get a visa for coming to America because of so many discrepancies in my documents; I had been denied a tourist visa three times by the American embassy and I was losing hope, I was even thinking of just breaking the marriage with my husband now if he would not be the one to come and join to live with me in the Philippines; it would have been easier for him to live in the Philippines than for me to live in America. But my husband was also more logical, his salary in America is about ten times bigger than what I was earning as a College Instructor in the Philippines. Out of hopelessness I decided to write an ideal scene, both written and collage ideal scene. My objective in the ideal scene was for me to live in America with my husband. Here's an example on how to write an ideal scene.

1. First you write the title in the present tense such as this:
2. "I am now living happily with my husband in America."
3. After writing the title in the present tense write

   "Ideal Scene" under the title
   Then write the details in the present tense like this"All the discrepancies in my documents are now resolved. I have now received my US visa. I am now living with my husband in Marion, Indiana, USA. We are now enjoying the consummation of our relationship as husband and wife. My husband is very nurturing and supportive to me and vice versa."

4. Then affirm such as this;

   "This or something better now manifests for me easily and effortlessly in very satisfactory and harmonious ways for the highest good of all concerned."
   In 2016 I had finally arrived here in the US and as I saw in my ideal scene everything worked perfectly in my marriage with my husband now.

Once your psyche becomes amenable to your method of manifesting, whatever method you use and whatever you wish in any area of your life, the Universe will dance and bow to your wishes. There is power within us that just awaits acknowledgment and exercise to make it work for us.

27

LIVING A PERFECT LIFE

What is a perfect life?

Is there such thing as a perfect life? Every person has a perfect life unique to him/her. What may be perfect for me is not necessarily perfect for anyone else; whether you agree or disagree is not important. Opinions have no place in a Universe where everything in this whole ecosystem is predestined by the Universal Law of Cause and Effect and more Universal and Natural Laws. Just like the Law of Gravity where, as an example, when you throw anything up it would surely come back down. Such is one example of the millions of Universal Laws that govern an individual life and all lives in general. Life can only be perfectly fulfilling when one lives the perfect life that is unique to him. But sad to say that per survey in all areas of life, 99.99% of the whole world's population are incapable of seeing much less experiencing the perfect life that is intended for each uniquely, in the individual level. Given the preceding statement, it sounds that nobody needs a perfect life. People define and study comprehensively success, happiness and the likes whether scientifically, theoretically, philosophically, by "trial-and-error", for what? Is it just to know and philosophize or theorize? Why not just live your own perfect life?

So, what then is a perfect life? The answer is for you to discover. The only rule is: Live the life that is unique to you... well find it first; start from within yourself, it's just there. Believe it or not, your choice.

Life is like a flower

"Life is like a flower, it blossoms as the sun rises but it withers at the end of the day." Needless to say, each of us is in this life for a predestined span of time. No one knows exactly when he is going back to the "Creator" to Mother Earth...or to the "Unknown"; but all of us know that the day comes as surely as the sun rises in the morning and hides at the end of the day. Given this premise, we can see that to have this individual life is a privilege or a gift rather than a right. What are you doing with your life? This gift? This privilege? Do you take care and develop it into its natural perfection? Or do you mess everything so that you are now living in the complicatedly entangled labyrinth hence not really living the life intended for you? Life means living, not mere existing. Living the life is its maturity and perfection. Maturity and perfection bear excellent fruits in various areas of one's life. On the other hand, mere existing is stupidly following what is right in front of him and what pleases the senses in a momentary basis; also trying to pleasure himself in a temporal yet potentially leading to the messy and entangled life. Politicians, professionals, authorities, church people, beggars, all sorts of people alike are sadly in this state of entanglements.

My perfect life. I personally discovered and established

the principles that govern my perspectives for a perfect life for me…find yours.

I live my perfect life with the following strategies;

1. I know my potentials; by just discovering my potentials is by itself an endless lifelong effort.
2. I establish my potentials as the foundation and basis for creating a framework that I religiously fill in towards the achievement of any goals that I have created in any given situation and stage of my life.
3. I developed my intuition, respect it and trust it then follow it sincerely in any given time and situation of my life.
4. I keep my eyes open for opportunities that fit my potentials, desires and dreams; I create opportunities if I don't find it in my present environment.
5. I check my desires, goals, dreams, plans, strategies, and the likes. Evaluate their validity, sincerity, quality as to whether they are destructive or creative and productive, negative or positive and so forth.
6. I trust myself fully and no amount of suggestions from anyone can defy the dictates of my intuition; I cannot be persuaded to do anything that detract from my life's perfect direction and I kick out any foolishness and entanglements that will lead to a problematic life. To elaborate each of these principles would mean writing volumes of books.

Living my perfect life is living consciously in a moment by moment basis and foreseeing those elements in life that don't belong to me. I know what I want for myself and I surely get it exactly as I want, in fact better. The only rule is; I only live the life that is intended for me according to my natural potentials. Everybody is born complete with potentials to live his unique perfect life. Yet, almost everybody dies a perfect xerox copy of all the miseries and entanglements of one another in a given environment and culture.

28

IT ONLY TAKES A SPARK: TO KEEP THE FIRE GOING

"It only takes a spark to keep the fire going." It was all too good to be true and whatever is too good to be true is oftentimes backed up with some creeping fears of "what ifs"...what if this situation that I am enjoying won't last? What if he will change? What if I am just living in a dream and suddenly, I wake up and ooops!

The house we rented was beautiful and new; three bedrooms three bathrooms, the spacious master's bedroom had a beautiful and spacious jacuzzi inside it. At the back of the house was a beautiful cottage for the servants. We had a stay-in housemaid named Lourdes who did all the chores for us in this wonderful house. My 14-year-old daughter Jean, my late husband Adrian and me were the only occupants in this house. The neighborhood was perfect; across the road was the Korean Mr. Kho, at the right over the fence was the American Mr. Fisher and on the left side was the Filipino Engineer Ratunel. My New Zealand-er (Kiwi) husband, Adrian Shiels was co-owner of three hotels. There were 16

Australians and New Zealand citizens who pooled together their resources to form a corporation then ran the hotel business in Balibago, Angeles City, Philippines; they ran three hotels there. I used to work as the bookkeeper and at the same time the manager for the Filipino employees in one of the hotels. But then there were lots of things, activities, and situations in the business that were contradictions to my values system. So, one day I had decided to leave the job; decided to "burn bridges".

In my core belief system was the conviction that I was a born teacher and/or a public speaker or lecturer. The job situation in the hotel had nothing to do with my accepted natural inclinations. I liked the money and the comforts of life alright but what about me? What about my "real me?" What about the "born teacher" that was screaming deep inside me? I had been a teacher since time immemorial; even when I was barely 9 years old, I was already a "Sabbath School Teacher" every Saturday for children's department in the church. It went on and on even when I was a Missionary/ Colporteur in the International Missionary Society.

To be working in a hotel especially patronized by sex tourist in our country was a great insult and challenge to my core values system. I had then realized that money and comfort in living is not all there is to satisfy the longings of the soul. Deep within me was a vacuum that demanded fulfillment; I cannot ignore me, I cannot ignore the "Self" which I call Senotiza, who screams for justice in her existence to this world. She always reminds me of who I really am and that I don't belong to the situation in my job; the prostitutes, the sex tourists, the vicious and lascivious clients that filled the hotel premises were not the types of people that I can tolerate to see in my everyday life. I remember the honor and dignity of the job that I had been into for years and years of my existence. Honor and dignity versus comfort in living and money without dignity is just rubbish for "Senotiza". There has to be a balance; honor+ dignity=money+comfortable life=fulfillment

It only takes a spark for us to be reminded of who we really are and then we burn bridges to separate us from everything that is not our personal reality. And once the fire starts burning then we will be back to our original state of existence. The most fulfilling and perfect life that each of us can choose to live in the individual level.

29

LIVING MY LIFE

What is the meaning of life?
A time for everything...

Songs of Solomon 3:1 has this to say;

"There is an appointed time for everything. And there is a time for every event under heaven."

When I was about 5 years old, my Dad left me and my 3-year-old little sister Lily in the house of my Auntie Tutay. She was older than my Dad and she was a Language Teacher, teaching Spanish in College. In one of our dinner time, for all the dinners that had happened during our stay in that family for about a month or so that our Dad left us, this was one of those very significant events in my experiences that left a mark in my belief system. There were lots of food on that long table. Our nine much older cousins whose ages ranged from 12 to 32, also surrounded that long table-full of variety of food. My sister and I were the "babies" and felt so tiny and insignificant in their midst; but they were very accommodating, loving and caring to us. My Auntie was a very jolly and energetic old lady and would always raise some thought-provoking questions. My sister and I only had one fried egg for each as compared to their crabs, roasted pork, fish, and name all the food, they got them, in all the dinner time that we were there. I can see how they enjoy all the food on the table. No, it was not because they were selfish that they did not share their food to my sister and me; it was because of my Dad's religion which was different from my Auntie and in which my Dad warned my Auntie never to feed us with "flesh food" while he was away. My Auntie knew what would happen if she disobeys my Dad...he was the brother with the worst tantrum in the family.

While everybody was eating, in which my 26-year-old-nurse cousin Benita, noticed me watching them eat sumptuously, asked me this question "Jenny, aren't you envious of us eating all these delicious foods while you and Lily only have that fried egg?" That question actually made me think; I was 5 years old but everybody would attest that I behaved like a matured person in my speech; they labeled me "little wonder girl" because of my questions that needed sincere and serious answers, especially from adults. My answer to Cousin Benita's question was "Papa said that if we eat fish and meat, especially pork, God will burn us in Hell." This answer caused some sort of provocation to all my cousins around but they were all considerate; but then Cousin Benita had this to say, "Our God is very kind and loving, He would never burn us in Hell no matter what we eat, for as long as the food is good and we enjoy them." This answer and a lot more probing on this subject between me and my cousins, convinced me of their sensible contentions. From then on, I started eating meat and would always question my Dad for any rules he would impose on us children, on me specifically. But since I was just a child, my Dad always won, at least for time being. In my adult life, my Dad found me very difficult to control because I had learned to live independently and I had learned to choose what to believe and live my life according to my own convictions. It all started from that dinner conversation when I was 5.

Living my life now
Just living my life
I had lived my childhood;
I had lived my teen years;
I had lived my youth;
I lived them in my every moment;
Nobody else lived my life for me;
But I learned from every person who came along;
Each of them doesn't need to be agreeable at all times;
But certainly, each had taught me a lesson or more;
That contribute to my being me in my here and now;
And even in my years to come.

30

LIFE IS BUT A DREAM: YESTERDAY, TODAY, AND TOMORROW

Yesterday

Yesterday was lived; We were all there, with the tiny shoes that we cannot wear anymore now; With the mother whose home is not our home anymore now; With the teacher we love or fear; With all the deeds, the fashion and style, the places, the people, and the things or objects we used to possess and enjoy. We just leave them behind with the passing of time, with growth and mobility that life demands us or expects us. Yesterday was lived and I have no regrets.

Today.

Today I count my blessings and thank the Great Intelligence for the life I enjoy today; Today is the fulfillment of the dream I dreamed yesterday; And because I am alive, I continue to dream; My dream for tomorrow will be my today as time passes by; Hence in my dream, I create my "today" for the kind of life I will have in my tomorrow.

Tomorrow.

Tomorrow will be my today How I dream and what dreams I have today will be my life in my tomorrow.

Life is but a dream Without the dream life has no direction and there is nothing to hope for; Without the dream, life is not life at all, it's just mere existence; And there will not be a today in our tomorrow; And we don't even have a "today". Did you live yesterday? If yes, then you live your "today". Yesterday is but a dream gone, today is a dream-creation for the kind of tomorrow that we dream of.

31

INTROSPECTION: SELF-APPRECIATION

Self appreciation is different from egotism. Appreciating ourselves and our lives is praising and thanking God for creating us and giving value to what God has done in our lives; whereas egotism, on the other hand is comparing yourself to others and becoming proud for the feelings and thoughts that you are better than them. Self-appreciation is simply acknowledging your value as a person, giving value to the reason that God has created you as a person and what you are going to do with your life.

The following is my self appreciation in an introspective form;

Nobody else can love me the way I do to myself.

Nobody else is with me in every second of my life.

I am the only living thing who is with me all the way since birth to present.

No one else knows me from inside out but me.

I am the only person who can know my feelings and my thoughts in any moment of my life.

I was there in every turn of my life and in every event, people, object, place that occur in every phase of my life. People come and go and so with relationships.

Money and all the material things I love that come with it all pass by.

Jobs and careers come and go.

Places I'd been have been left behind so I can move to one that suits me and my needs in a given time; but in all these, I am still with me and I am the one who knows and experiences all the thoughts and the feelings involved in every occurrence, in every step, and in every phase of my life. I know myself better than anyone else could know about me; therefore, I am the only person who can love me and accept me completely as I am.

Nobody will eat the food for me when I am hungry.

Nobody will study the lessons for me so I can pass my exams when I was a student; and so forth and so on.

Nobody feels the grief for me when my husband died. Nobody cries for me for my lose and even if they do, I would still grieve and cry for myself.

My parents loved me completely but they loved me because I am their child and they have dreams for me which I probably cannot dream for myself. Sometimes they are around but not all the time and every time I needed them.

My husband loves me because I am his wife who he may be happy and proud about and whose company he can enjoy with, for his certain needs but I cannot know exactly what is in his mind and in his heart, and vice versa.

I have flaws, I make many mistakes, I made wrong decisions, I fail on many of my dreams and aspirations; even love ones criticize me and point their fingers on me, friends and lovers may prove untrue and all the unfairness in life may happen and no one may stand by me but I have my Self, my reliable Self who forgives all my mistakes and flaws and who is sincerely compassionate of my weaknesses.

The Self that assures me that everything passes by and that every moment is a moment of revival and of coming back to the "Self" who truly knows me;

I am the one who knows why things happen the way they do in my life and so I can always change course when things go wrong.

No one else can make major decisions for me when it comes to my life's destiny. I am my own perfect decision-maker for myself because if I make wrong decisions, I am the one who suffers most. I love my self;

I know that I am a wonderful creature and I am capable of handling my own life to make it better and better and better in all aspects. Whatever other people say against me do not bother me because I know who I am.

People may judge me according to their measure but I accept myself completely as I am and I allow myself to explore life according to the guidance of the "still small voice" that speaks to me in every turn of the way.

I trust that voice inside me; it is the one who had been with me all the way it is excellently reliable; I see my own truth and reality and I like it;

I love everything that I am, that I do and that I possess.

I love my self completely as I am, including my pains, my flaws, my mistakes, my failures, my hardships, my difficulties, my struggles and endeavors.

I trust My Self completely and I never betray "Me".

No one else can understand and accept me completely

as I do my self. I have no other life; this is me and I cherish myself;

I cherish my precious life so I don't allow anyone to affect me.

If I am not 100% for "Me" through and through, will anyone be for me all the way?

No, they have their own self too to attend to.

32

THE PROCESS OF
SOCIALIZATION

Man is a social being and "no man is an island." Human beings cannot stand alone normally without other humans to mold him and fit him into a certain society and the world as a whole. What you are at present is the by-product of who you had been in the past and your gene, your perception and interaction with the whole Eco-system that raise you from birth to present. Each personality is an accumulation of the complex cultural influences and his natural and inherent tendencies in any given condition and phase of development. No one has the right to judge anyone else because we are all different from one another both inherently and socially. Matthew chapter 7 in the Bible says something very significant about judging others "Judge not so you won't be judged; for whatever mete you measured to others will be measured back to you." We all differ on who and what type of people we had mingled with in our development and these people have very strong impact and influence in the way we behave and in our decision-making activities. This is also the reason of the adage "tell me who your companions are and I will tell you who you are." Personally, I had made some introspection on who I had been with in the past and I had grouped them into the following: Classifying and grouping the people I had normally mingled with and encountered in my whole life

1. Parents, siblings, children, husband/s, and other "heart relationships" (family and loved ones)
2. Servants and employees
3. Peer groups
4. Clients
5. Sales people
6. Employers and Big Bosses
7. Students
8. Social groups
9. The Public

There could be more but these are the basic and major people that are found in my horizon; I can write volumes of books if I will write for each of them.

The adage "Tell me who your companions are and I will tell you who you are" is a perfect statement to measure the type of personality we had become. Are you sociable? Shy? Introvert? Extrovert? Ambivert? Candid? Secretive?

Whether we agree or not or whether we are aware of it or not, each of us is a byproduct of both our inherent and hereditary qualities and the socialization processes we had been into which in turn include the total socioeconomic-demographic and the complete cultural values system we come from or had been through and which we had accumulated over the years. The English anthropologist, Edward Tylor defined culture as "a complex whole which includes knowledge, belief, art, law, morals, customs and any other capabilities acquired by people as members of a society." These are just few of what a person deems important in the core of his personality and are demonstrated in his behavior, decision-making, and lifestyles, among others. We are mainly what we are now in the personality level and in our socialization and interpersonal relationships because of what we had been through in all aspects of cultural influences and what kind of people we had been socializing with; and these are in addition to our inherent qualities.

Whether I like it or not and whether I am aware or not, each group of people have great impact of who I am now.

Family and loved ones- I am the first born, and not to mention that I was born at the time when my Mom and Dad had lost their hope of ever having children after 21 years of marriage without having any child of their own, hence it is but normal that I got all the attentions, love and adoration from my parents and the admiration of my two siblings that followed me. I had to be good, my parents had high expectations from me because I should be the role model of my two younger siblings. They both measure up to me in any of their endeavors in life. And my family was small. This family setting and my place in the family has a big impact in my character and personality, I tend to become an achiever and feeling loved and worthy of admiration. I carried out this character and personality even in choosing and handling my love life relationships in my later years. I had an inherent attitude of "If you love me, you're lucky and you have to be faithful to me because if you hurt my feelings I will instantly kick you out from my life, that's easy for me to do because I don't need you, I am the one needed, I am not in need."

Servants and employees: The household servant or what we locally call the "maid"

I always had a maid since time immemorial. In my childhood both my parents were busy in their respective businesses and preoccupations during the day so that we had all types of servants to run the household and to baby-sit us when we were kids. Whether throughout my marriage life and when I was living alone, I always have at least one maid to do the chores, hence having a maid is not a luxury for me, it's a necessity because my mind and time is always busy with something else. If I were to count how many maids had come my way ever since, I would say they won't be less than a hundred; hence I have a fairly good comparison of the types of personality of these people. I should be more understanding even with their false pride and self-assessments. I am tolerant to them to a certain extent.

It would be a very long story if I will have to explain each of the group of people that I had associated in the past which contributed to who I am in my present; the bottom line is our characters, personality and even temperament are molded by the types of people that surround us in a given time and place and most of all by our socioeconomic standing in a given environment and society.

Hence know the types of people and their characters and values system that surround you, they are the mirrors of your personality and the kind of life that you live.

33

JUST A LITTLE GLIMPSE
OF LIGHT

The following narrative poem was a symbolic expression of my true feelings when life was so hard to bear. Life is wonderful, never boring, there are twists and turns and turning points that happen along the journey of development. Anyone who would say that his life is boring because there is nothing significant that happened to him is not really living his life; he just exists. We have to acknowledge and embrace every situation that we had been into. To embrace life is to feel every given situation, be it blissful or hurting. To embrace joy and happy experiences encourages repetition of that blissful moment and is actually an act or a ritual to summon more wonderful things to happen again in our lives. To embrace sad, hurting and difficult life situation that we had been into reminds us that we are fallible humans, that we make mistakes hence this acknowledgment will make us better persons once we get out from such situation; it also reminds us the essence of the statement "this too will pass" therefore we can summon courage to keep us through, it will make us bolder to face any life situation and new ventures; and when success happens it reminds us not to be boastful because nothing is permanent in this life.

Here's my expression at the darkest moment of my life:

Just a Little Glimpse of Light

Groping in the cold and the seemingly unending darkness that encompasses this particular night of my soul; in the cold night when I was lost for some confusing reasons;

My heart longed for the Light, just a glimpse of light to guide me home;

To the home where merry hearts and abundance in everything good thrive;

Where Love and praises to the beauty of this Universe and its Creator warms every soul;

My limbs are numbed from the cold;

My heart is painfully pounding for the fear of the dark;

Such darkness where a monster might appear to devour me into pieces;

In this darkness where no one exactly knows what evil might happen?

Who can rescue me from this horrible situation and condition?

I cannot even see; everything is just darkness and I don't know where I am; not a step would my numbed and painful legs do;

Where is home?

Where are my parents who care for me?

Do they remember me?

Do they know that I am lost?

If so are they going to look for me and eventually find me?

It seems like eternity in this condition;

I had been crying too long and quietly, afraid to even scream, otherwise the evil ones might be the first to hear me;

I long for home;

Just thinking of the comforts in my home gave me some strength;

I just need some glimpse of light now;

I can see how important the Light is, now that I am lost in this darkness;

Then suddenly a little light is moving…just a dot of light is wonderful to follow in a darkness like this;

As I crawled to follow the Light, I realized that it grows bigger and it continued to move as if guiding me;

As the Light increased its brightness, I started to see the grasses that surrounded me and I remember where this place was;

I knew where I was and I knew what direction I should be going;

This knowledge alone was enough to provide me strength to carry on; if it was just to crawl towards the comforts of my home.

34

THE MAGIC OF TURNING YOUR WORRIES INTO CREATIVITY

Have you ever met any person who had never feel worries once in a while in all his life? Everybody, in one way or another and in certain degrees, had have worries in life. Even the seemingly jolly and successful person is carrying in his head certain worries that he often is not aware of. The year 2008 was my third year of teaching back in SPCC main campus; I had left my post as the Chair in the College of Business Administration, AWOL in 1999 when I realized how sick my late husband, Adrian Shiels was. He needed 100% attention because he was on oxygen throughout the two years that he was bedridden. When Adrian died in 2003, I suffered depression and was sulking in grief inside my bedroom without going out from the house for a year. My friends and colleagues thought that I had left the country because I warned all my family members not to tell anyone of my whereabouts, "how bouts" and "what bouts." Actually, I was not completely sulking, my heart and mind cannot hold for too long all these painful negative thoughts and feelings. During the interim I had bouts of depression, sadness, worrying, discouragements and losing my desire to live. I was 50 and among my negative self-inflicting thoughts were the weakening will and the loss of desire to live any more. Among my worries were my being out of job, being broke and in my age, nobody will hire me and I lost any source of income. My son was married already with three small children and my daughter was still in College as a working student in SPCC.

Remembering my reality Then I remember the adage "Necessity is the mother of invention." Necessity, yes, that was the situation in my family; there was a dire need for a change and yet I cannot figure out what I could do to ease the needy condition that we all were in. Realizing the situation, I still didn't exert any outward effort to change the situation, rather I started to remember who I am. The first thing I did was, I just got my pen and notebook, my colors, my white bond papers then started writing everything about who I really am, my skills, my profession, my education and so forth; then followed by writing down what I deserve in life and draw them in the bond paper.

The Twist I had been doing all these introspection and self-assessments in the one year that I was sulking inside my bedroom. Then one day out of the blue, the billionaire lady, Mrs. Jojo Haynes, came to visit me. She learned about me through my daughter-in-law. I never knew her at the time and had never heard of her let alone her socioeconomic status. She had been looking for a person who have my educational status and skills. At first, I refused to accept her offer and her request for my help concerning her undergrad thesis in AB Psychology. She had already hired a PhD to do her thesis but she failed and had wasted one year to do it all over again. The offer was a salary equivalent to my professional fee as a Chair in a College plus such benefits as housing me in an expensive three-bedroom condominium in Manila, complete with a housemaid, a modern automatic car with its driver, free complete three meals a day, among others. I still refused the unusually attractive offers; it was just too good to be true for me. But her persistence, six times coming back to me, finally impressed me; it was unbelievable that this rich lady was having such high regard of me and with such 100% trust on me and my capability, so that I accepted the offer eventually. I cannot help myself asking why. Did my affirmation "I, Jenny, now have a satisfying and well-compensating job." written 20 times every day in first, second, and third person and within two months' time, work? I just knew one thing. I changed my mind from worrying to creating, even in the mental and "writing" efforts only. What was truly amazing was, after working satisfactorily with Jojo by which she passed top one on her thesis, er the thesis I made for her and my coaching, I received lots of job offers and even SPCC, where I left my post five years ago without a leave of absence nor asking or telling anyone that I was leaving my post, rehired me.

SPCC again So, in the third year of this come back; Atty Robert John Donesa, the HRD at the time would be seen sitting in my office every morning when I arrived at work. I asked him why he would do that when his office was located several buildings away from my office; His answer was "I would like to know your secrets on why you are not affected with all the problems and gossips and politicking's in this school." I just smiled and said, "I just know how to turn worry into creativity."

35

ACKNOWLEDGING THE IMPORTANCE OF YOUR VALUES SYSTEM

What is Values system and how does it govern your lifestyle?

On people, sheep, and snail:

People are likened to a herd of sheep and to a snail.

Sheep must herd together and must follow one another; or a sheep must follow the butt of the one closest to its eyes, otherwise it will go astray and will get lost for good. Sheep, by nature, are short-sighted; they don't have to think independently they just follow blindly and that is all that they have in all their lives.

Similar to sheep, people are social beings too, they need one another to base the direction of the individual life, to warm their hearts, to inspire mental activities and attitudes, and perhaps to put colors into their lives; these are only among the other complex reasons to need other people. There is nothing wrong if people are liken to sheep being social beings but to base completely your lifestyle with the rest of the people surrounding you would mean that you are short of using your God-given ability to think and respect your personal desires to better yourself.

Similarly, a snail is cold so that it will need another snail or anything to warm its body and whoever or whatever is closest to it regardless of qualification and quantification, to warm its life. Like a snail, people are normally warmth and molded by the nature of its belonging to a social group or environment, subculture or the culture as a whole. But human beings are given the choice, unlike snails, people have the inherent ability to choose the kind of life and culture that could inspire them, and they should live in the individual level.

The difference between people and these lower forms of animals, is that, humans are endowed with the ability to think, they can choose what to think, they can qualify and pre-qualify the nature of their thought processes, and they are far above in the nature of their intellectual capacity which, when compared to brutes, can be unlimited if they choose to.

To think is to rationalize in which one questions the validity and values of an idea or a premise. The following are some questions if answered in the core of your being, could lead to finding within yourself what values system dominates your flow of thinking.

What do you value most in your life?

How much do you value your job?

Given a specific situation, "Which is more important to you, the job you have in a given time or a certain relationship that may have conflict with such job?"

In terms of values system, I would like to quote the

biblical verses to the effect as follows; "…do not worry about your life, or about your body…on what to eat, what to wear, what to drink…the body is more than food and clothing… the birds and the lilies don't worry and work but are fed and are arrayed with beauty;…people are more of value than the birds and the lilies…worrying cannot change things.."

Value yourself more than anything else and base your all your Values System on this idea.

By nature, human beings are supposedly far higher in value than anything natural and man-made in this world. What you value most is the most important thing that could affect the quality of your life in any phase. Anyone in an individual level, who can see the essence of these statements, could have a much better life than any of those unwanted situations that one is in, in the personal level. Just straighten out your values system. You can do that; you are naturally equipped with such ability, just search it within you and once you found it then you will be courageous enough to discover and live the life you deserve.

36

LIFE IS MOBILITY PLUS VARIETY 03/02/17

Among my favorite philosophical quotes is Heraclitus'
"No one steps on the same river twice." I was in my
MAE (Master of Arts in Education) Philosophy class in
1988 when I first encountered this statement. My instant
question was, why did he say this? Of course, at that time
my normal way of thinking could not see the logic of this
statement, I can always step on the same river a million of
times if I so desired. There was no answer for me at that time,
theorizing and philosophizing were shallow justifications to
that statement.

I had to live years more when Heraclitus' statement
recurs every now and then in which it gradually unfolds
and makes sense in my mind; it helps me understand certain
present situations in a given time as I live my life on.

The river has a natural current that keeps flowing and
pushing downward towards the direction of the ultimate
body of water, the sea or the ocean. The next time you

step on it, it won't be the same water you had stepped on previously.

Similarly, life has several "currents" that keep it moving. But unlike the river where the flow is just downward and coming from just one direction which is from a higher ground, "currents" in life come from various directions and can go astray, upward, downward, side-ward or is sidetracking to nowhere in a variety of forms and degrees. Most often if one is not aware of it, and always the case for those who understand the workings of the psyche, the strongest currents come from within the person and these forces or currents invite allies from outside forces to strengthen and perpetuate its natural tendency.

To cite an example

Among the millions of complexities and varieties of "currents" or forces that cause one's life to move is either the lack or the excess of money; along with money is what money can buy and where money comes from. Again, in a variety of reasons, money is a constant in every person's mind and life eventually. One major reason though, is that money is a tool to make the quality of living better or worse, depending on its availability in one's life and on the degree, variety, complexity, number among others, of the "current", needs or desires to be met for a certain individual in a given time.

How money become a current or force that move my life

My sight, my smile and eating (teeth), my breath, my health, among other parts of my body are necessary for my existence and enjoyment in life. Without money and the source of money (people, loved ones) that care enough for me to live normally then I won't have life now; it would either be literally dead or just existing.

A river or a body of water that had sidetracked from the main river because of a flood and some other reasons, and which had stayed in that new location, will eventually either stink, discolor and become a habitat of deadly bacteria (therefore detrimental to the environment and its inhabitants particularly people), for being stagnant or just dry up through evaporation on the air and the heat of the sun. It is not a river anymore but an offshoot, a dead offshoot.

I would have been blind, toothless and ugly, famished due to selective eating being toothless, and worse, just exist counting the days of short and difficult breathing condition till breath would completely run out; dead.

These names will live on with me; Rey, Ronald, Greg. I call them the extension of my life; their pockets are their investments, not to mention their love. Rey is my son and my sight, Ronald is philanthropist friend and my smile, and last but not the least, Greg is my hubby and my heart and breath.

Can you follow how the river flows, ere, the direction of my thinking? From Heraclitus to my life, the current lives on or the forces live on. The formula is just an integral part, if not implied.

37

MY LIFE'S JOURNEY

The following narrative poem is my personal journey in terms of relationships. Humans as social beings need company in this life. Those who have been into romantic relationships know that life is more beautiful, colorful and meaningful when they have someone who deeply love and care for them. But what happens to your life when this someone is gone from your life by any reasons? There is a saying that goes "It's better to have loved and lost than never to have loved at all."

Another saying that catches my attention is "there is always someone for each of us." Nothing is permanent in life. People in your life come and go, even your children grow and they go with their own lives to live, money come and go, properties and possessions come and go, your youth come and go. What remains is your life and everything that is you in a given time, body, soul, and spirit for as long as you are still alive.

Even the spouse you married and you stay married till death is not the same person you first married, there are a lot of changes between the two of you including the quality of your relationship, good or bad, there is always a change to both of you in the personal level.

My own experience in terms of relationship is when my partner is gone through death or simply separation due to personal incompatibility that we discovered along the way, the longest time that I have no one to love me is two years then another one come along to offer me company. I personally know of many women who don't desire to have a partner in life anymore after the hurting break-up they experienced in their previous relationship or for other reasons that they alone can see. Some of them have secret longings to experience love again but they just cannot find the person that they think would match their personality or that meet their desired partner in life.

For these women I would suggest…get deep within yourself and discover what you really want. If there is hatred within your heart or some phobia for having another person in your life face it by affirming "I love myself completely as I am including all my flaws. I am a loving and lovable person. My perfect mate comes to me easily and effortlessly" If you do this consistently somebody will again knock on your door and would offer love and companionship to you.

Here's the poem…

I walk along the highway of a life time journey;

I started with both my parents and siblings walking side by side with me;

Together we walked in life's wide road; with spirits high in hope, faith, love and security.

For whatever reasons, I suddenly found myself walking alone;

My parents and siblings went their own ways, to each his own;

I wanted to turn back and trail them; But I was confused whose road to follow;

For each was trailing a road apart from one another.

I screamed to them to wait for me;

Or for them to follow the road I take, but they obviously never heard me;

Instead I heard a voice which said;

"Follow your own path and stick to it." And when I tried once more to look their way;

Before my eyes they just faded away.

I am so lonely and afraid now that I am all alone on this wide and dusty road;

I know not what to do; I just know that I have to move on;

Hoping that somewhere along the way; our paths would meet and we will be together once more.

And so I walk on with a heavy heart;

When I notice that someone else is walking beside me;

He holds my hands as he says "Fear not; I am with you.

"In my confusion I welcome him; for is it not that in this journey, two is better than one?

I need his company, or any good company in this journey.

He seems to be attentive to my needs;

He provides me food when I am hungry and water to quench my thirst;

He shields me from the cold and from the rain and even from the biting heat of the sun;

He helps me to take another step onward when my legs are tired and weary;

And carry me with his strong arms when I cannot make it on my own;

For all the good things that he does to me;

How can't I be convinced that he is my perfect mate throughout this endless journey?

We continue to walk together as we move on in this life's pathway;

This time I carry our daughter while he holds our son who walks beside him;

My joy and confidence cannot be contained for having a family of my own walking with me;

The stranger that used to be is now the loving father of my children.

But then life's journey has twists and turns and ups and downs;

Sometimes the road splits in two or more;

And when I turn to look, I find out that one is missing along the way.

We are walking with my two siblings in this journey for decades more;

Now I realize that It's just my grown-up children and I walking in this journey;

And now I walk on with my children by my side; With hearts full of hope for the bright home ahead;

But once again in life's hi-way; there are always crossroads and twists and turns;

Until I find once again that my company is another stranger;

The stranger who finally walks home with me.

38

LIFE IS A SERIES OF INDIVIDUAL CHOICES

A happy outlook and a positive disposition in life brings blessings and attracts good luck.

Love lifted me.

When difficult times in any area of our existence seem to hover in the horizon of our lives, my Mom used to sing this; "I was sinking deep in sin (oblivion and confusing situations) far from the peaceful shore; Buried deeply stained within, sinking to rise no more; But the Master of the sea heard my despairing cry; From the waters lifted me now safe am I. Love lifted me..."

In any given situation in our lives where some gloomy conditions appear along life's journey and that we had done our best, yet what we aspire for still fails or did not meet our expectations, then we had two choices to make; we can choose to despair and accept ourselves as losers in life or, we can choose to know and affirm our true value as dignified human beings. "When nothing else could help, Love lifted me" was another song that inspired me ever since my childhood to this day. When everything else fails and nothing else could help, all I do is to remember who I am. Remembering who I truly am then counting my blessings and affirming my true state of being and the wholesome experiences with God and the Universe have actually made my life flow easily even amidst life's "tempestuous waves." Such collective experiences during family devotional hours impressed in me positive outlook in life which had become the strong foundation that our parents had instilled in us siblings.

A family that prays together stays together

Some people tend to despise those who adhere to some religious practices in the family. They seem to forget that, as the smallest social unit, the strength of a family relationship goes a long, long way throughout life's twists and turns. They would brand religiously-inclined people or their siblings as being brainwashed. Strong family foundation generally makes a person strong when he goes through life's journey on his own in later years. Family religious practices such as praying together during devotional hour and going to church together are a blessing to a few family if done in the spirit of family fun; being together or in unity and family camaraderie, rather than being imposed by the parents as the only way to get to heaven, must be the essence of religious practices in the family. Fanaticism should be deliberately discarded.

Effects of my religious background to my outlook in life My siblings and I had developed strong self-value and high self-esteem because of the strong foundation we had experienced during our childhood. In the process of personal growth and development, I had discovered a pattern for myself which I lived by. I can sense when things are not going right so that I can take charge of my life and choose what path to follow. When things really go wrong to the extent that I sometimes feel like everything seems to be out of my control, then I pray and meditate; this is my refuge, the source of my strength. Prayer and meditations, or praying and meditating are habits, hence they would have started early on in life; this wholesome and powerful habit normally originates from family practices. Lots of people talk about meditating but they just cannot do it consistently; they need to effort to develop the habit. Any person who try to analyze me according to their shallow and acquired way of thinking, may say anything, negative or positive, that they perceive about me but nothing can affect me whatsoever because I know exactly who I am and I know that only me and my God can know who I am. No one else can know me and everything there is to know about me, better than I do; hence no one and nothing can run me down nor let me down except when I allow it to happen. Remembering who I am and my "power" within that emanates from the Source of all Intelligence and which I had learned from an early age to be working for me, fades away or banish any negative influences from the wickedness of any human. I am protected by the Divine Guidance and Providence.

My affirmations about myself...a positive outlook, a daily meditation...

This is me; This is my life;

No one else can live my life for me in every second of it; I appreciate everything that I am, everything I do, and everything that I acquire and possess; I have a reliable power within me that works for me in every turn; This power within me is my inherent gift from the Origin of all Powers and Great Intelligence that Governs Natural Laws; When in difficulty and when nothing else could help; This power within me lifts me up and raises me to a higher ground; If I fail in one area of my life then I can turn and choose to focus on those where I am good at; The deeper I sink into oblivion, the higher also I rebound; Remembering this principle and pattern of my life brings me back to my true state of being.

These or something better now manifest for me easily and effortlessly in very satisfactory and harmonious ways for the highest good of all concerned.

39

I Am: "I Think Therefore I Am"

I am sharing here the philosophy of existence...let those who have brains understand, those who have eyes see and those who have ears hear...

"I Think Therefore I Am"

I borrow this statement of Rene Descartes for the title of this hub. This hub is actually a poem I created springing out from the bottomless vacuum of human existence. The title of this poem is "I Know You" and here it goes;

"I Know You"

You authentically exist, I acknowledge you; in fact, you had been long in existence eons before I come out to this physical world;

The wind carries you swiftly with a lightning speed from nowhere through all the four dimensions of the Universe and the four corners of this globe;

You were there very long before the Great Wall of China had been conceptualized by those who came to and went off in the land of the living;

You watched the advent of civilization and how it flourished in the Niles as it advanced towards the so-called New Age of human existence;

You are lulled to sleep by the melody of angels singing their praises of love and beauty to the "Alpha and Omega", the Almighty no-beginning and no- ending HIM;

In the Land of Nowhere where the Universe dance and sing with the myriads of bejeweled stars and the whole of the planetary family, you are there too, celebrating festively;

You swim and wade in the infinitely wide and deep blue oceans of the endless depths somewhere, yes somewhere;

The seven times heat of Nebuchadnezzar's oven is nothing compared to your billions and trillions and even measureless voltage;

You are Omniscience, everywhere and anywhere, every-time and anytime, somewhere and someway, and anyhow and anyway;

You are clad with the infinitely colored brilliant beauty and the glaring gleam of once upon a time Lucifer's priceless gems;

Your Being You is beyond telling by any fallible human like me but I know you.

In all of your wanderings and adventures with the brightness and brilliance of everything sprouted and created and with the timelessness of your perfectly aesthetic existence, one day you came to a halt, an impossibly abrupt halt;

You were suddenly tasked for a mission to accomplish

in order to prove the authentic relevance and purpose of your existence;

The Order came to you as a complex mixture of complete and lingering darkness, a thunderous and boisterous sound of the unknown and the nowhere, a lightning speed and glare from a throne beyond the blue;

You are trapped!

You stumbled to the abyss of no escape;

Escapade is only possible when the mission is accomplished with flying colors of honor and glory;

Or you can hate your situation enough to abort the mission in your own volition;

No rewards for such choice, only punishments; for forever you will be disdainfully ugly and be eternally exiled to the infamous cell of eternal imprisonment and damnation for the King of Tarsus, the once upon time Lucifer, whose choice was to reign in the throne of endless discomfort, to say the least;

Countless of the inhabitants there were like you and they made their choice to go against the Will, against the Order;

You are vacuumed in confusion; You want to scream but to whom? You want to move but how?

This is a totally different ground you are in; Your power is limited in this vacuum;

You needed to be connected to the Land of Nowhere where you had been;

You are trapped inside the Crown of Creation, Me!

A lot of those like me do not acknowledge the likes of you in them; and it bothers me a lot;

I want to reach out to them and tell them to take heed to the one who dwells in them;

How can I be understood?

But you must be persistent inside me;

Your scream within me is so loud, you won't let me sleep unless…unless, I recognize you and listen to you;

I listen to you and I had been listening since I acknowledge your authentic existence in me;

I know you because you are Me.

40

DEAR GOD: A SUPPLICATION TO THE UNIVERSAL FORCE

There are times in our lives that we find ourselves so angry and feeling hatred to some people and situations that caused us harm hence draining our energies. Anger is a very powerful feeling that if not controlled will cause us so much trouble; when left unresolved it can accelerate to hatred which then lead to behaviors to avenge ourselves that could hurt others too, even the innocent ones. Even the bible says "Love your enemies..." a statement that is so hard to follow and which most people could only pretend but not really loving the enemies from the heart. This kind of feeling happens when we feel we are being mistreated and being betrayed by the very people who are supposedly important to us, the negative feelings multiply and can eventually block the blessings that should have been intended for us hence life become a curse. Following is a prayer that could help us ease this feeling. This is also a prayer for protection so that nobody can hurt you and your feelings. Let God and the Natural Laws of the Universe do what is good for you when you are pestered by this kind of destructive emotional state.

Dear God, Heavenly Father, where are you? I feel so lost but I remember your promise to me being your precious child in this Universe that you created and love.

In my meditations, I clearly "hear" your voice saying; "Ask of me and I will give you whatever your heart desires."

In you Oh Lord do I put my wholehearted trust;

Uphold me in your Loving-Kindness;

Pamper me in your Infallible Righteousness; and catapult me to a safe ground.

Incline your ears to my woes and let me experience your Divine Guidance.

You are my Strength, my Pillar and my Stronghold;

My Rock, my Fortress and my Refuge whose powerful words command the whole Universe to protect me from harm.

Save me Oh God from the claws of the wicked;

Snatch me from the hands of blood thirsty men whose days are spent on self-destruction and causing misery to others in the process.

You are my All-knowing Almighty Father who upholds me even when I was in my mother's womb;

You brought me out to this life to channel your Divine Love to those around me;

You are my Hope and Assurance in my youth;

You are always here within me and with me in every twist and turn in my life's path ways;

I honor and glorify you in my mind, in my heart, in my soul and in my whole life through;

You are my Foundation; All praises to you Heavenly Father for as long as I live.

I am my earthly father's delight and my mother's angel;

I am a wonder to many who know me personally;

All these are only true because you are my Father in Heaven who empower me;

Because You are a Living Fountain in my heart;

You actually live the life that I am living now;

My wisdom is yours;

My words are Yours in my mouth;

My love for my love ones and humanity as a whole is Your love for them that you allow me to live upon;

In my whole life, all praises are for you my Father in Heaven;

You stand by me and protect me when my faith in life and men fails me.

Where I am weak, you are my Strength.

My enemies may speak evil against me; they prowl and betray me;

They lie to me with their devilish schemes and they counsel among themselves against me saying; "Her God has forsaken her; let's pursue and shame her for there is none to save her."

But vengeance is Yours my Father;

You know who they are and where You find them;

Let them be confounded and consumed;

Oh my God! make haste to avenge me!

Let those who seek to hurt me, be filled with reproach and dishonor.

But for me, I will praise You and honor You more and more continuously throughout my life;

My heart rejoices with the melody of your angels' voices that ring deep in my soul;

My mouth shall only speak and tell of your Great Faithfulness and Your pure Righteousness all the days of my life;

I always live my life in the Strength and Power of my Almighty Father;

The Strength and Righteousness of the Lord endures forever;

His Righteousness protects me against the evildoers.

Oh God! You had taught me Righteousness even in my youth;

To this day and to all the coming days that You had made for me, I declare Your wondrous works in my life.

In my old days you fill me with your wisdom and power beyond fallible human understanding;

They can only surmise on Your Godhead and Righteousness, but are they there yet?

Their ignorance, disbelief and dishonor to your Power bring themselves suffering as a consequence.

Your Righteousness O God is very high;

You perform miracles in my life;

Had shown me great wonders;

You lift me up to the highest pedestal in my life's station;

You bring me peace when I should have been in the den of the devil;

You snatched me out from the brink of death and hell;

You continuously and untiringly increase my greatness and comfort me in every twist and turn of my way;

With the music in my heart and with the melodious

pulse beats of my blood, I praise your Faithfulness to me Oh my Heavenly Father.

My God! You are my miracle.

The unfathomable Love of my life.

You lift me up above the ordinary;

My tongue speaks only your Truth and your Righteousness all the days of my life.

I praise You Oh God for avenging me from the lying tongues and the evildoers;

They are now confounded and they cause themselves disgrace; dishonor;

Humiliation is their destiny.

Oh God! Who is like You in my life?

41

TWO INNER REFLECTIONS: MY THOUGHTS AND MY PRAYER

Only Good Thoughts dwell in my mind.

I had written down two powerful reflections on January 16, 2001. I say powerful because they really worked for me. It was the time of my life when my husband was bedridden and on oxygen; I knew it won't be long that he would go back to the Creator, but I needed strength to sustain me as I took care of him. He died two years later; if I reflect now how I did it, I can see the enormous strength I had to take care of him full time; leaving my job and care-giving him from the smallest details till the end; for three years.

Here they are.

My Thoughts

Moment by moment, second by second;
Minute by minute, hour by hour;
Day by day, night by night;

Week by week, month by month; In every tic-tac of the clock is a moment of <u>thoughts</u>.

Now, this moment, is my only and perfect time for thinking of everything that is fine;

I think good and of good things only;

I think of good feelings;

I think of love and compassion;

I think of joy, delight and pleasure;

I think of all-natural beauties;

I think of God, the Source of "all things bright and beautiful"

I think of abundance and riches in this wonderful Universe;

I think of forgiveness and peace;

I think of the goodness in humans;

I think of all the pleasant and comforting words, live them, and speak them;

I think of good deeds for myself and for others;

I think of my service for my Lord and for all His creatures who need me;

I think of myself as God's channel of love and infinite creative energy and wisdom;

I think of all the wonderful things in this Universe and of riches untold;

I think of all the mysteries in the secret chambers of man's existence that are yet to unfold;

I think of all that man can think and create;

I think of all the wonders of man as God's "crown of creation" and masterpiece;

I think of God's unconditional love to all mankind;

I think of everything good that is manifesting to me this very moment;

I think and I think, and no matter how I think, I know that my mind never stops thinking, so I choose what I must think;

And these are only good thoughts for the good of all concerned.

These are my thoughts, this very moment.

My Prayer

Give me a <u>heart</u> that knows no ill;

Give me a clean and pure heart Oh Lord;

Impute in me the <u>mind</u> that thinks only good for everyone and for myself;

Grant me understanding, discernment and <u>wisdom</u>;

Endow me with a healthy and strong body which reflects your own and that can be of service for the weak and the weary.

Reflect in me your love, kindness and compassion for my children, my love ones, and for those who are bereft of the essence of life's joy;

Inculcate in me peace, meekness, mercy and grace to model your Greatness in my everyday life;

Let me fathom life's <u>reality</u>;

Allow me to envision creativity and presence of mind to model a fulfilling life;

Unfold me to the peak of my God-given energy and enthusiasm in order to accomplish and achieve my life's goals and purpose;

Empower me with a systematic and logical approach to life's challenges that I may meet along life's journey.

I praise you Oh Lord for all the good things that you let me partake;

I count all my blessings, piece by piece, with such rejoicings in my heart;

I acknowledge you as the only Source of everything that I enjoy in life;

You granted me all the desires of my heart and you continue to fulfill your promise of meeting all my needs in perfect timing at all times;

Whatever I asked in your name is done unto me;

How Great You are in my life Oh Lord;

I desire to proclaim You and your Goodness to those who are yet in the dark;

You are the Light when my path is cloudy;

You carry me with your powerful arms when I am unable to move on my own;

My faith in you gets stronger as you continue to show me the wonders of living;

You reveal to me what is hidden beneath the seeming catastrophe of life;

Great is Your Faithfulness Oh Lord!

What you had done for me in the past is the same today and through eternity;

You had given me everything to live a fulfilling life in all areas;

Whatever I ask and pray for is already granted me, and even those I had not thought of asking due to my limited vision, you had already given me.

How Great You are Oh my Lord!

I humbly offer myself and my life to you My Lord, just as I am;

I give you my mind, my heart, my body, and all that I am;

I give you my love, my faith, my trust, my loyalty;

There is nobody else in this vast universe who is worthy of my praises and thanksgiving;

For I know that that You had given yourself to me even before I was conceived in my mother's womb;

And you are the Source of my life which I gladly offer to you in return;

Make me your trustworthy steward to perform the task you assigned me in this life;

Let me execute my talent in full capacity;

Mold me into a channel of your Divine Love and Power;

Let me be the inspiration for others to live their lives according to their individual Divine purpose;

I do everything for your glory and honor, Oh Lord.

I now claim the blessings that you intend for me today.

Thank you, Father.

These do I pray. Amen! And Amen!

42

PURGING AND CLEARING TECHNIQUES

Do you wonder why no matter how you follow the techniques I had presented; nothing still happens and there are no changes in your situation? The techniques of affirmation, collage and drawings are very effective to manifest your desires only, and only if you are clear from anything that blocks your energy to reach your subconscious mind or that psyche that makes things possible for you.

Purging and Clearing Technique

These two words may sound strange for some if not most readers but in this article I am modeling a type or technique of clearing your hearts, mind and soul from the spiritual, emotional and psychological rubbish that you have accumulated and stocked over the years in your "mental cabinet" within you thus blocking your energy from manifesting what you really desire and deserve to happen in your life.

Do you often wonder why no matter how you try or do your best you just fail to get what you really want or to actualize your dreams or to achieve your goals? Situations in your life such as financial difficulty, entangled relationships, non-challenging job, and even some perennial feelings of emptiness, among others, continue to repeat in a spiral manner in every turn of your life. These repeated and continuous nuances should be cleared out and completely eradicated from your life in order for you to develop towards the completion of your being here in this life. Life should be lived and be alive rather than just going along struggling and coping with whatever comes your way till the end.

Living your life is a process and a series of choices from the smallest daily decisions such as whether to say yes or no and what dress to wear when a friend suddenly invites you to an unannounced casual dinner; or a major decision such as to abort an unwanted pregnancy or to keep the pregnancy going for nine months that may change your life completely because such decision would lead to another major decision affecting your job, income, relationships, etc. Life should not be a continuum of a "problem-solving" nature; it should rather be a continuous series of "creative" nature where every moment is a moment of creativity and a wholesome exploration and adventure in any areas.

No matter how seemingly brilliant and successful a person is in all his endeavors, if these rubbish are vacuumed in his core, then the time will come that it will just be one more "miss-take" for him and everything he had worked hard for will blow up and tumble down before his eyes.

Given all the preceding argument as valid, the following are two of some actual effective techniques I used in the spirit of fun; I am still using these when necessary:

1. Clearing through forgiving technique
2. Purging Via Inner Exploratory Conversation.

Forgiving Technique;

Writing a letter

In this technique I write down the name of the person who hurt me today or yesterday or in the nearest past; one person at a time. Then I write him a letter, the following is a simple example;

George, (husband)

"You hurt me deeply. You yelled at me and called me an idiot, an ignorant, worse you lie to me and betray my trust in you. You cheat on me by having an affair with another woman yet you continue to lie and deny your wrong doings. Your betrayal to our marriage vows hurt me to the core and is draining my energy having lost my enthusiasm to function normally.

But now I made the decision, I am dissolving all these restricting energies that block me from my personal progress. I have to forgive you; I am forgiving you now. I forgive you and I let go of all the blocks between us. I forgive you now; go your way as I go mine. I now bless you."

Then I read the letter as I ponder on its truthfulness; feel the hurt in the area where the hurting point is mentioned and allow myself to cry if I feel like crying. Then I feel the relief where the letting go is mentioned. Finally, I tear the letter and burn it or throw it to the rubbish as a gesture of completion, then forget about it. Having accomplished something brings a feeling of relief.

Purging: Inner Exploration

In this technique, I am writing down an inner

conversation with myself concerning matters that are bothering me in the present. I have named my inner self Senotiza. The following is an example of our conversation:

"Me (Jenny): Senotiza, what's bothering me?

S (Senotiza): Hmmm, no formal address to me? Can't you be a bit polite?

Me: I don't even want to live anymore (expletives if you wish), what can be polite do with my disgusting life now?

S: At least be civil.

Me:9 Sh…(expletive) answer my question.

S: And if I won't?

Me: And why won't you? What's the use of your existence in me?

S: Hey Jenny, what's boiling you now?

Me: Am so mad because I bought some lottery tickets today and I never won anything.

S: Wowooo! Lottery tickets huh…!

Me: Yes, because I want to be a multimillionaire.

S: Hehehe…hahhaahahahah…aren't you being funny?

Me: Sh…don't laugh at me, I am serious!

S: Serious in winning the major lottery jackpot or serious in becoming a multimillionaire? C'mon stop kidding me.

Me: Both, I want to become a millionaire by winning the lottery.

S: In that case, you are limiting your chances to become a millionaire, whereas if it's the becoming a millionaire you focus on, you will have less frustrations.

Me: But I cannot think of any way to become an instant millionaire.

S: Just because you cannot think doesn't mean that there is no other way. What about just pretending that you are already a millionaire? By the way, why would you want to be a millionaire? What are you going to do with such huge amount of money?

Me: Hmmm…I just want to experience having plenty of money, something like no matter how I spend, and my money is still intact.

S: Could be but what if you got your wish granted, do you have anything specific in your mind to spend on?

Me: Yes, first I will share my blessings to my daughter; she is now building a house so I'd love to contribute in the amount of P2M, then I also give her another P1M to buy her car and whatever she wants. I love my daughter and I want her to enjoy some goodness in life. Then my husband and I will travel within a year around the globe, hopping from one country to another, living in luxury hotels and resorts and meeting all my friends around the globe. I will introduce my husband to them. My husband had been working all his life and he is very generous to me; he deserves the goodness in life. I want him to spend the rest of his life with me full of joy and a fulfillment."

S: Hmmm…noble objective…go on, just continue imagining what you do with your money. I will be right back with some surprises for you.

There would be a lot of topics, more serious ones if you wish, in this type of inner conversation in the personal level. The idea is that you will discover what you really want and you will know from within you those things that are holding you back. It is okay to explore impossible areas. An idea or answer will just come out and you will be surprised when you will be opened to many possibilities.

Just do this exercise in the spirit of fun. Life would never be boring once you had learned to adapt this technique in your daily life.

The only rule here is; just do it, don't ask questions.

43

Smile, Laugh, and Be Lucky

Do you laugh a lot? Why and what make you laugh? Your own thoughts momentarily? Your feelings in that particular time? Or, is it anything you hear, see, touch, read, smell, said, among others that make you smile this certain moment? People are a bundle of varied and diversified emotions. These emotions may come in a surge or as a reaction to any given environmental stimulus in a particular time and situation or occasion.

All of us had experienced all these emotions in any given moment of our life. Emotions are intangible but demonstrable through our behavior or action in a given moment. Some observable show of emotions may be smiling, laughing, crying, lashing, screaming, yelling, kissing, hugging, the list can go on and on. Is it the company of someone you fully trust, love, care and with whom you had been familiar for a long time that you just blurt into laughter spontaneously with just a slight provocation in a positive and funny sense for both of you?

But the question is; of all the emotions you have experienced which ones are making you feel good about yourself and about your relationships and about life as a whole? Or do you think that emotions have definite bearings in how your life is going in all areas?

How does a habitual spontaneous smiling and laughing attitude attract good luck?

1. Lady Luck cannot resist a merry heart. It's been said that "Fortune is a lazy goddess, she will never come to you." But Lady Luck cannot resist a merry heart and this merry heart must be loud enough for Lady Luck to hear, must be bright and glaring enough for Lady Luck to get curious about hence be drawn to you, and must be a full-packed action of wholesome and habitual behavior for Lady Luck to stick with you.

2. Habitual and spontaneous laughter in intimate relationships magnetizes Lady Luck. Studies had shown that couples and family members for that matter, who laugh a lot together for any reason, or even for seemingly no reason at all are the ones who stick together and they are inseparable. It's the laughter they share together in a habitual and spontaneous manner that draw them together even in the midst of difficulty, griefs and problematic situations. So you get "Lucky" in your relationships.

3. Lady Luck bows down to a persistently bright and shining smile and to a thunderous and spontaneous laughter. A person who notices any humor in little things in life can easily smile and laugh hence develops wholesome and bright dispositions even

in a most difficult situation. So, he gets "Lucky" eventually.

Some scenario

I am going to share some experiences here to prove my point; to show how my smile and laughter invited Lady Luck to my horizon. I was younger but already married and having two children in which my eldest, a son, was aged 7 and my daughter, the youngest was aged 4. It was my first year of teaching in a Public High School wherein new teachers were receiving a monthly pay of P1,337. At that same time I was also studying in MSU-IIT (Mindanao State University - Iligan Institute of Technology) taking up my MBA as a scholar. I used to drop by in my best friend's eatery before proceeding to my 6-9 MBA p.m MBA schedule. I had to have a quick snack; I was famished from my 7-5, 8-hour daytime teaching job. My best friend at that time was Becky, she owned and ran the Hamburger House; this was the place I frequented every 5-5:30 p.m. during the workdays and before proceeding to my MBA classes in MSU-IIT. Becky and I used to laugh a lot together, oblivious of whether people noticed our behavior. In one of my appearance there after school Becky told me that those two guys sitting in one of the tables wanted to be introduced to me. Naturally I declined; I am not good at strangers and I easily lash at people when a hint of disrespect drops in my ears. But Becky, being my trusted longtime friend assured me that these guys were decent and they just had to ask me some important questions. We had ten minutes of good introductions before I left for school. Before leaving, Engineer Recto, one of the two guys and who happened to be the Superintendent in one of the departments in National Steel Corporation, told me; "Jenny, you got that winning smile and that sharp brain, can we talk some time about a job offer in National Steel Corporation?" In this I answered "Try me."

The job offer was a three-hour Motivation Lecture every Sunday. I was paid P1,500 per hour which means I was receiving P4,500 every Saturday which means P18,000 a month. Compared to my P1,337 per month salary teaching in public school, P18,000 is a fortune, and to top it all, I didn't have to leave my main job of teaching in a public school because I was only giving lecture 3 hours in the weekend, a Sunday. It all just started with a smile and the habitual attitude of smiling even in a slight provocation.

A smile conveys a positive vibe to the observers. National Steel Corporation was the biggest Steel Corporation in Asia at that time and I was employed as a Motivational Lecturer. This is just one of the many experiences of good luck in my life that had started with just a smile.

So, smile, laugh, and Good Luck.

44

EPISODES OF DARKNESS

Let's face it; Life is not always bright and gay. In fact, it is full of confusion and gloom; Lots of those we dread are the ones that are in our immediate situation; We try to cope and try to shine to fade the shadows away; No effort is needed to be in the dark; you're just there. But to shine and to be in the Light requires constant and consistent alertness and assertiveness. The following is an expression of my feelings during a dark moment for some reason. Acknowledging your emotions even the negative ones will remind you that you are living your every moment and that you are capable of loving and accepting yourself no matter what.

Following is an expression of my darkest moments; I entitle this

"Leave Me Alone!"

Leave me alone!
Don't tell me you care for me

All of you! Don't ask me where I had been and what I had been doing;

Why do I have to explain defensively, you don't believe me anyway!

You cannot and won't do what I want, why should I?

I cannot tell you that I had gone to meet the Devil in Hades;

It's not fun to be with him but his proximity is everywhere;

You can access him any moment any place. Just one "mis-step", one mistake and he's there to meet you.

I should have desired to be in the glorious throne of the Heavenly King;

I should have loved to hear the voices of angels singing their Hallelujahs to the Universal Power and the Almighty!

But it's too far away, I even have no idea where it is and can it be real?

Ha-ha, foolish people, foolish me! I don't care anymore;

I don't care about anything;

Leave me alone in my miseries;

Stop adding insults to my injuries.

Forget me if you will;

Remind yourself that I don't exist and never had been in your life.

Let me be a wanderer in the limbo of this so-called life of the living dead!

45

HOW TO CREATE A LASTING PERSONAL HAPPINESS

Given that the premise "The only way to enjoy lasting happiness is to live the life you personally created for yourself..." is true; I created some suggestions on how this works in the individual level. This idea is an abstract from the indisputable fact that "everything that exists, both natural and man-made, is the solidification and functions of a creative mind." I had personally applied this method to myself and found it to be very effective; I just want to share my experience, who knows it may also work for you.

1. Discover those things, types of people and relationships, events, and activities that lift up your spirit or that excites you naturally;
2. Make a list of at least ten items in each category of the ones mentioned above;
3. Rank and prioritize the items in your list, starting from most priority down to the least;

4. Pick one from each category; the ones that dominate most your thoughts and feelings in almost all your present moments;

I could add a hundred more items to the list but for the purpose of just showing an example, I pick only four items to work on.

An example Discovering myself;

After making some mental revisiting my past concerning those "happy moments" of my life, I had decided on the following as among the ones that make me smile just by thinking of them.

Activity 1
1: Listing down 10 things that I love to do;

1. Creating my paper houses and other handicrafts such as crocheting, sewing, embroidery
2. Writing down my true feelings in a given moment maybe a story, a beautiful experience or a dream or aspiration
3. Listening to wholesome and favorite music, singing, composing lyrics of a song, dancing alone or with a group of good friends
4. Drawing or sketching or painting
5. Socializing, speaking or being surrounded by an audience of wholesome, attentive and appreciative people
6. Visiting and exercising or doing physical activities such as calisthenics in the gym;
7. Swimming in a pool or a river or the beach

8. Taking photographs of natural beauties, innocent babies, flowers, and many things that I perceive as beautiful and worth-preserving

9. Hiking or walking, down parks, highways and most especially by a beautiful riverbank, cool mountaintop that overlooks a village, blossoming wild flowers in a wide green meadow at a valley or plateau and walking by the beach;

10. Pedaling a bike around a wholesome and opulent subdivision

Activity 2:

Listing down 10 (people) types of people and relationships that lift up my spirit;

1. My son and his beautiful children
2. My daughter and her lovely family
3. My husband
4. My best friend
5. Seeing old friends like Mina, Becky, Betty, Fredy, Raul Escobar, Ronald, Neneng
6. My Dad and Mom
7. My Sister and Brother with their families
8. Some of my favorite ex-colleagues like Nayding, Odette, Ma'am Grace, Ma'am Shirley, Ma'am Orfi, and new acquaintances of their likes that they introduce to me etc.
9. My cousins Selfa and Silvici
10. My biological mother Esperanza

There could be more such as job, education, career, leisure and travels, places. The idea is you should recall all those things, people, events, places and things that you possess and that they actually made you happy in the past and at present and you sure will also be in your future.

Now using the two categories in the example above;

For the first category I take number 5 as number one in the rank and this is what I strongly feel as my immediate need. "Socializing, speaking or being surrounded by an audience of wholesome, attentive, happy, appreciative and inspiring people."

Then my next choice to rank number one in the next category should jibe with my rank one in the first category so I pick number 8. In this I realize that my immediate need is a career similar to what I had when I was with them that could uplift my spirit. Or, it could be that I need to have a job again in another setting and that my happiness would be when I socialize with wholesome people in a wholesome setting.

Realizing this particular need in a given time, then I would know what to do. Following are some possibilities;

1. Contact my daughter or Ma'am Veron, my best friend or any close friend within my proximity;
2. Arrange a party and tell them to invite their friends;
3. Create a viable reason for the party, something that convinced them of your being an attractive, if not irresistible friend.
4. Prepare an agenda to make the party alive.

This party may be free, sponsored, or you spend for everything. The idea is to discover your immediate need and create a situation to meet such a need. Don't include financial problems in planning a situation like this; you will be surprised that ideas and resources present themselves once your mind is made up.

There could be more activities such as while alone working on your favorite hobbies such as drawing or sketching and painting or creating some handicrafts that you enjoy doing.

Okay. That's all for now; Good Luck! Fill your days with happiness, workout for it.